James Otis: The

by John Clark Ridpath

Near the northeast corner of the old Common of Boston a section of ground was put apart long before the beginning of the eighteenth century to be a burying ground for some of the heroic dead of the city of the Puritans. For some quaint reason or caprice this acre of God was called "The Granary" and is so called to this day. Perhaps the name was given because the dead were here, garnered as grain from the reaping until the bins be opened at the last day's threshing when the chaff shall be driven from the wheat.

Here the thoughtless throng looking through the iron railing may see the old weather-beaten and time-eaten slabs with their curious lettering which designate the spots where many of the men of the pre-revolutionary epoch were laid to their last repose. The word cemetery is from Greek and means the little place where I lie down.

In the Granary Burying Ground are the tombs of many whom history has gathered and recorded as her own. But history looks in vain among the blue-black slabs of semi-slate for the name of one who was greatest perhaps of them all; but whose last days were so strangely clouded and whose sepulchre was so obscure as to leave the world in doubt for more than a half century as to where the body of the great sleeper had been laid. Curiosity, whetted by patriotism, then discovered the spot. But the name of another was on the covering slab, and no small token was to be found indicative of the last resting place of the lightning-smitten body of James Otis, the prophetic giant of the pre-revolutionary days. He who had lived like one of the Homeric heroes, who had died like a Titan under a thunderbolt, and had been buried as obscurely as Richard the Lion Hearted, or Frederick Barbarossa, must lie neglected in an unknown tomb within a few rods of the spot where his eloquence aforetime had aroused his countrymen to national consciousness, and made a foreign tyranny forever impossible in that old Boston, the very name of which became henceforth the menace of kings and the synonym of liberty.

Tradition rather than history has preserved thus much. In the early part of the present century a row of great elms, known as the Paddock elms, stood in what is now the sidewalk on the west side of Tremont Street skirting the Granary Burying Ground. These trees were cut away and the first section of the burial space was invaded with the spade. Tomb No. 40, over which the iron railing now passes, was divided down as far as where the occupants are lying. Within the sepulchre were several bodies. One was the body of Nathaniel Cunningham, Sr. Another was Ruth Cunningham, his wife. The younger members of the family were also there in death.

When the lid of one coffin in this invaded tomb was lifted, it was found that a mass of the living roots of the old strong elm near by had twined about the skull of the sleeper, had entered through the apertures, and had eaten up the brain. It was the brain of James Otis which had given itself to the life of the elm and had been transformed into branch and leaf and blossom, thus breathing itself forth again into the free air and the Universal Flow.

The body of the patriot had been deposited in this tomb of his father-in-law, the Nathaniel Cunningham just referred to, and had there reposed until the searching fibres of another order of life had found it out, and lifted and dispensed its sublimer part into the viewless air. Over the grave in which the body was laid is still one of the rude slabs which the fathers provided, and on this is cut the name of "George Longley, 1809," he being the successor of the Cunninghams in the ownership of Tomb No. 40.

Here, then, was witnessed the last transformation of the material, visible man called James Otis, the courageous herald who ran swinging a torch in the early dawn of the American Revolution.

The pre-revolutionists are the Titans of human history; the revolutionists proper are only heroes; and the post-revolutionists are too frequently dwarfs and weaklings. This signifies that civilization advances by revolutionary stages, and that history sends out her tallest and best sons to explore the line of march, and to select the spot for the next camping-ground. It is not they who actually command the oncoming columns and who seem so huge against the historical background--it is not these, but rather the hoarse forerunners and shaggy prophets of progress who are the real kings of men-- the true princes of the human empire.

These principles of the civilized life were strongly illustrated in our War of Independence. The forerunners of that war were a race of giants. Their like has hardly been seen in any other epoch of that sublime scrimmage called history. Five or six names may be selected from the list of the early American prophets whose deeds and outcry, if reduced to hexameters, would be not the Iliad, not the Jerusalem Delivered, but the Epic of Human Liberty.

The greatest of these, our protagonists of freedom, was Benjamin Franklin. After him it were difficult to name the second. It is always difficult to find the second man; for there are several who come after. In the case of our forerunners the second may have been Thomas Jefferson; it may have been Samuel Adams; it may have been his cousin; it may have been Thomas Paine; it may have been Patrick Henry; it may have been James Otis, the subject of this monograph.

It is remarkable to note how elusive are the lives of many great men. Some of the greatest have hardly been known at all. Others are known only by glimpses and outlines. Some are known chiefly by myth and tradition. Nor does the effort to discover the details of such lives yield any considerable results. There are great names which have come to us from antiquity, or out of the Middle Ages, that are known only as names, or only by a few striking incidents. In some cases our actual knowledge of men who are believed to have taken a conspicuous part in the drama of their times is so meagre and uncertain that critical disputes have arisen respecting the very existence of such personages.

Homer for example--was he myth or man? The Christ? Where was he and how did he pass his life from his twelfth year to the beginning of his ministry? What were the dates of his birth and death? Shakespeare? Why should not the details of his life, or some considerable portion of the facts, compare in plenitude and authenticity with the events in Dr. Johnson's career?

It seems to be the law of biography that those characters who are known to the world by a few brilliant strokes of genius have as a rule only a meagre personal history, while they whose characters have been built up painfully and slowly out of the commonplace, like the coral islands of the Atlantic, have a great variety and multitude of materials ready for the hands of the biographer.

James Otis belonged to the first of these classes. There is a measure of elusiveness about his life. Our lack of knowledge respecting him, however, is due in part to the fact that near the close of his life, while he was oscillating in a half-rational condition between Andover and Boston, with an occasional visit to Plymouth, he fell into a fit of pessimism and despair during which he spent two days in obliterating the materials for his biography, by destroying all his letters and manuscripts. He did as much as he could to make impossible any adequate account of his career or any suitable revelation of his character as developed in his correspondence. Over and above this, however, the materials of his life are of small extent, and fragmentary. It is to his formal publications and the common tradition of what he did, that we must turn for our biographical and historical estimate of the man. In this respect he is in analogy with Patrick Henry who appears only fitfully in history, but with meteoric brilliancy; or with Abraham Lincoln the narrative of whose life for the first forty-five years can be adequately written in ten pages.

The American Otises of the seventeenth century were of English descent. The emigration of the family from the mother country occurred at an early day when the settlements in New England were still infrequent and weak. The Otis family was among the first to settle at the town of Hingham. Nor was it long until the name appeared in the public records, indicating official rank and leadership. From Hingham, John Otis, who was born in 1657, ancestor of the subject of this sketch, removed to Barnstable, near the center of the peninsula of Massachusetts, and became one of the first men of that settlement. He was sent to the Legislature and thence to the Council of the Colony in which he had a seat for twenty-one years. During this period he was promoted to the place of Chief Justice of the Common Pleas, and while holding this important place he was also judge of the Probate Court. The family rose and flourished in reputation.

In 1702, James Otis, son of Judge John Otis, was born. He followed in his father's footsteps becoming a lawyer and colonial publicist, afterwards a colonel of the militia, a judge of the Common Pleas, a judge of the Probate Court, and a member of the Council of Massachusetts. Just after reaching his majority Colonel Otis took in marriage Mary Alleyne, and of this union were born thirteen children. The eldest was a son, and to him was given his father's name. It was to this child that destiny had assigned the heroic work of confronting the aggressions of Great Britain on the American colonists, and of inspiring the latter to forcible resistance.

James Otis, Junior, was born at a place called Great Marshes, now known as West Barnstable, on the 5th of February, 1725. He inherited from his father and grandfather not only a large measure of talents but also a passion for public life which impelled him strongly to the study and solution of those questions which related to the welfare of the American colonies, and to the means by which their political independence might be ultimately secured.

The character and intellect of Colonel Otis of Barnstable were transmitted to other members of his family also. The daughter Mercy, oldest sister of James Otis, was married to James Warren who made his home at Plymouth. This lady had her brother's passion for politics--an enthusiasm which could hardly be restrained. She wrote and conversed in a fiery manner on the revolutionary topics of the day. Almost coincidently with the Battle of Bunker Hill she composed and published (without her name, however,) a biting satire on the colonial policy of Great Britain, calling her brochure "The Group." Fifteen years afterwards she published a volume of poems, mostly patriotic pieces, and finally in 1805 a brief "History of the American Revolution," which was considered a reputable work after its kind.

Samuel Alleyne Otis, youngest brother of James, outlived nearly all the other members of the family, and was recognized as a prominent political leader. He, also, had the strong patriotic and revolutionary bent of the family, was popular and influential, and was honored with a long term of service as Secretary of the Senate of the United States. In this capacity he participated, April 30, 1789, in the inauguration of Washington, holding the Bible on which the Father of his Country took the oath of office. The other brothers and sisters were of less conspicuous ability, and were not so well known to their own and other times.

In New England in the first half of the eighteenth century the sentiment of education was universal. Among the leading people, the sentiment was intense. Colonel Otis, of Barnstable, was alert with respect to the discipline and development of his children. He gave to them all, to the sons especially, the best advantages which the commonwealth afforded. James Otis was assigned to the care of Reverend Jonathan Russell, the minister at Barnstable, who prepared the youth for college. By the middle of his fifteenth year he was thought to be ready for matriculation. He was accordingly entered as a freshman at Harvard, in June, 1739.

Of the incidents of his preceding boyhood, we know but little. A tradition exists that he was more precocious than diligent; that his will was strong; that his activities were marked with a reckless audacity, which, however, did not distinguish him much from the other promising New England boys of his age. Something of these characteristics are noticeable in his college career. At Harvard he showed an abundance of youthful spirits; a strong social disposition, and a well-marked discrimination between his friends and his enemies. At times he applied himself assiduously, and at other times mused and read rather than studied. On the whole he did not greatly distinguish himself as a student. His passion for literature was marked, and he became conspicuous for his forensic abilities. Towards the end of his course, his character as a student was intensified, and he was not often seen away from his books. Out of term time, he would return to his father's home taking his books with him. At such times he was rarely seen by his former companions of Barnstable, because of his habit of secluding himself for study.

It is narrated that at this period of his life, young Otis gave strong evidence of the excitable temperament with which he was endowed. In the intervals of his study his nervous system, under the stimulus of games or controversial dispute, would become so tense with excitement as to provoke remark. Nor may we in the retrospect fail to discover in this quality of mind and temper the premonitions of that malady which finally prevailed over the lucid understanding, and rational activities of James Otis.

The youth did not much effect social accomplishments. He had a passion for music and learned to play the violin. With this instrument he was wont to entertain himself in the intervals of study. Sometimes he would play for company. It was one of his habits to break off suddenly and rather capriciously in the midst of what he was doing. Thus did he with his music. It is narrated that on a certain occasion while playing by invitation for some friends, he suddenly put aside the instrument, saying in a sort of declamatory manner as was his wont--

"So fiddled Orpheus and so danced the brutes."

He then ran into the garden, and could not be induced to play the violin again.

Young Otis passed through the regular classes at Harvard and was graduated in 1743. On that occasion he took part in a disputation which was one of the exercises of his class. Otherwise his record at the college is not accented with any special work which he did. At the time of his graduation he was in his nineteenth year. It had been his father's purpose and his own that his profession should be the law. It does not appear, however, that his college studies were especially directed to this end. At any rate, he did not devote himself at once to the law, but assiduously for two years (1743-45) to a general course of study chosen and directed by himself with a view to the further discipline of his mind and the widening of his information. It was an educational theory with Otis that such an interval of personal and spontaneous application should intervene between a young man's graduation and the beginning of his professional career. Having pursued this course with himself he insisted that his younger brother, Samuel Alleyne Otis, should take the same course. In one of his letters to his father--a communication fortunately rescued from the holocaust of his correspondence--he discusses the question and urges the propriety of the young man's devoting a year or two to general study before taking up his law books. An extract from the letter will prove of interest. The writer says: "It is with sincerest pleasure I find my brother Samuel has well employed his time during his residence at home. I am sure you don't think the time long he is spending in his present course of studies; since it is past all doubt they are not only ornamental and useful, but indispensably necessary preparatories for the figure I hope one day, for his and your sake, as well as my own, to see him make in the profession he is determined to pursue. I am sure the year and a half I spent in the same way, after leaving the academy, was as well spent as any part of my life; and I shall always lament I did not take a year or two further for more general inquiries in the arts and sciences, before I sat down to the laborious study of the laws of my country.

"My brother's judgment can't at present be supposed to be ripe enough for so severe an exercise as the proper reading and well digesting the common law. Very sure I am, if he would stay a year or two from the time of his degree, before he begins with the law, he will be able to make better progress in one week, than he could now, without a miracle, in six. Early and short clerkships, and a premature rushing into practice, without a competent knowledge in the theory of law, have blasted the hopes, and ruined the expectations, formed by the parents of most of the students in the profession, who have fallen within my observation for these ten or fifteen years past."

The writer of this well-timed communication then adds in proof of his position, the names of several distinguished jurists who postponed the beginning of their legal studies, or at least their legal practice, to a time of life quite beyond the conventional student period. Mr. Otis then declares his conviction that a young man may well procrastinate his legal studies until he shall have attained the age of thirty or even of forty years. He declares his belief that such postponement will as a rule lead to better result than can be attained by a youth who begins at twenty, however brilliant his genius may be.

This view of the case was with James Otis both theory and practice. He began his legal studies in 1745. In that year he became a law student under the tuition of Jeremiah Gridley who at that time was already regarded as one of the most able and accomplished lawyers in Massachusetts. Preceptor and student were at the first in accord in their political and social principles. At the time of the young man's law course, Gridley was a member of the General Court of Massachusetts. He belonged to the party called Whig; for the political jargon of Great Britain had infected the Americans also, and they divided according to the names and principles of the British partisans of the period.

Judge Gridley, while he remained on the bench, took sides with the colonists in their oncoming contention with the mother country. Afterwards, however, by accepting the appointment of Attorney General he became one of the king's officers, and it was in this relation that he was subsequently brought face to face with his distinguished pupil in the trial of the most remarkable case which preceded the Revolutions.

Mr. Otis devoted two years of time to his legal studies before beginning the practice of his profession. The study of law at that time was much more difficult than at the present day. The student was obliged to begin de novo with the old statutes and decisions, and to make up the science for himself by a difficult induction, which not many young men were able to do successfully.

Law text-books were virtually unknown. Otis did not even have access to "Blackstone's Commentaries." No authoritative works on evidence or pleading existed in the English language.

The student must get down his Acts of Parliament, his decisions of the King's Bench, his Coke, his black-letter dissertations on the common law, and out of these construct the best he could a legal system for himself. To this work Mr. Otis devoted himself from 1745 to 1747, after which he left the office of Judge Gridley and went to Plymouth, where he applied for admission to the bar, and was accepted by the court. He began to practice in 1748--the year of the treaty of Aix-la-Chapelle, when the political and historical status of Europe was again fixed for a brief period.

The young attorney almost immediately took rank at the Plymouth bar. The old records of the court at that place still show the frequent appearance of Otis for one or the other of the parties. In this manner were passed the years 1748 and 1749. It does not appear that at this time he concerned himself very much with the affairs of the town or the larger affairs of the commonwealth. The tax records show his name with an entry to the effect that in 1748 he estimated his personal estate at twenty pounds besides his "faculty," by which was meant, his professional value.

A few incidents of this period in Otis's life have come down by tradition. He soon made a favorable impression on the court and bar. He gained the good opinion of his fellows for both ability and integrity of character. This reputation he carried with him to Boston, whither he removed early in the year 1750. He had already acquired sufficient character to bring his services into requisition at places somewhat distant from Plymouth.

His reception in Boston was accordingly favorable. Beyond the limits of the colony he became known as an advocate. He was sent for in important cases, and showed such signal ability as to attract the admiring attention of both court and people. Already at the conclusion of his twenty-fifth year he was a young man of note, rising to eminence.

There was good ground for this reputation in both his principles of conduct and his legal abilities. From the first he avoided the littleness and quibble which are the bane of the bar. He had a high notion of what a lawyer should be and of the method and spirit in which he should conduct his cases. He had as much dignity as audacity, a sense of justice as keen as the purpose was zealous in pursuing it.

It came to be understood in the courts of Boston when Otis appeared as an advocate that he had a case and believed in it. He avoided accepting retainers in cases, of the justice of which he was in doubt. Pursuing this method, he was sometimes involved in law-suits in which he was constrained to turn upon his own client.

The story goes of one such instance in which he brought suit for the collection of a bill. Believing in his client and in the justice of the claim, he pressed the matter in court and was about to obtain a judgment when he accidentally discovered, among his client's papers, a receipt which the plaintiff had signed for the very claim under consideration. Through some mistake the receipt had again got back into the man's possession, and he had taken advantage of the fact to institute a suit for the collection of the claim a second time.

Seeing through the matter at once, Otis took the plaintiff aside, confronted him with the receipt and denounced him to his face as a rascal. The man gave down and begged for quarter, but Otis was inexorable; he went back to the bar and stated to the court that reasons existed why the case of his client should be dismissed. The court, presided over by Judge Hutchinson, afterward Lieutenant-Governor and Chief Justice of Massachusetts, expressed its surprise at the turn of affairs, complimented Otis for his honorable course as an advocate, commended his conduct to the bar, and dismissed the case.

With the spread of his reputation Mr. Otis was summoned on legal business to distant parts. On one occasion he was called to Halifax to defend some prisoners under arrest for piracy; believing them to be innocent he convinced the court in an eloquent plea and secured the acquittal of the prisoners.

On another occasion he was summoned to Plymouth to defend some citizens of that town who had become involved in a riot on the anniversary of the Gunpowder Plot. It was the custom in the New England towns to observe this day with a mock procession, in which effigies representing the Pope, the Old Bad One, and James the Pretender, were carried through the streets to be consigned at the end to a bonfire. In this instance violence was done by some of the participants; windows were smashed, gates were broken down, etc. Mr. Otis conducted the defense, showing that the arrested persons taking part in a noisy anniversary, and committing acts that were innocent in spirit, if not innocent per se, ought not to be adjudged guilty of serious misdemeanor. This plea prevailed and the young men were acquitted.

It is to be greatly regretted that the legal pleas and addresses of James Otis have not been preserved. A volume of his speeches would reveal not only his style and character, but also much of the history of the times. The materials, however, are wanting. He kept a commonplace book in which most of his business letters of the period under consideration were recorded. But these give hardly a glimpse at the man, the orator, or his work. Tradition, however, is rife with the myth of his method and manner. He was essentially an orator. He had the orator's fire and passion; also the orator's eccentricities--his sudden high flights and transitions, his quick appeals and succession of images.

To these qualities of the orator in general Otis added the power of applying himself to the facts; also the power of cogent reasoning and masterful search for the truth which gained for him at length the fame of first orator of the revolution. The passion and vehemence of the man made him at times censorious and satirical. His manner towards his opponents was at times hard to bear. His wit was of that sarcastic kind which, like a hot wind, withers its object.

All of these dispositions seemed to increase his power and to augment his reputation, but they did not augment his happiness. His character as an advocate and as a man came out in full force during the first period of his Boston practice; that is, in the interval from 1750 to 1755.

On attaining his thirtieth year Mr. Otis came to the event of his marriage. He took in union, in the spring of 1755, Ruth Cunningham, daughter of a Boston merchant. From one point of view his choice was opportune, for it added to his social standing and also to his means. From another aspect, however, the marriage was less fortunate.

The Cunningham family was not well grounded in the principles of patriotism. The timid commercial spirit showed itself in the father, and with this the daughter sympathized. The sharp line of division between patriotism and loyalty had not yet been drawn --as it was drawn five years afterward. But it began to be drawn very soon after the marriage with serious consequences to the domestic peace of the family.

It appears that beside this general cause of divergence, the staid and unenthusiastic character of Mrs. Otis rather chilled the ardor of the husband, and he, for his part, by his vehemence and eccentricity, did not strongly conciliate her favor. There were times of active disagreement in the family, and in later years the marriage was rather a fact than a principle.

The result of Mr. Otis's marriage was a family of one son and two daughters. The son, who was given his father's name, showed his father's characteristics from childhood, and certainly a measure of his genius. The lad, however, entered the navy at the outbreak of the Revolution, became a midshipman, and died in his eighteenth year. The oldest daughter, Elizabeth, went wholly against her father's grain and purpose. Just before the beginning of the Revolution, but after the case had been clearly made up, she was married to a certain Captain Brown, at that time a British officer in Boston, cordially disliked, if not hated, by James Otis. Personally, Brown was respectable, but his cause was odious. He was seriously wounded in the Battle of Bunker Hill. Afterwards he was promoted and was given a command in England. Thither his wife went with him, and Mr. Otis discarded them both, if not with anathema at least with contempt.

It would appear that his natural affection was blotted out. At least his resentment was life-long, and when he came to make his will he described the circumstances and disinherited Elizabeth with a shilling. The fact that Mrs. Otis favored the unfortunate marriage, and perhaps brought it about-- availing herself as it is said, of one of Mr. Otis's spells of mental aberration to carry out her purposes--aggravated the difficulty and made her husband's exasperation everlasting.

The younger daughter of the family shared her father's patriotism. She was married to Benjamin Lincoln, Jr., a young lawyer of Boston, whose father was General Benjamin Lincoln of revolutionary fame. The marriage was a happy one, but ultimately clouded with honorable grief. Two promising sons were born, but each died before reaching his majority. The father also died when he was twenty-eight years old. The wife and mother resided in Cambridge, and died there in 1806.

The second period in James Otis's life may be regarded as extending from 1755 to 1760; that is, from his thirtieth to his thirty-fifth year. It was in this period that he rose to eminence. Already distinguished as a lawyer, he now became more distinguished as a civilian and a man of public affairs.

He caught the rising interest as at the springing of the tide, and rose with it until it broke in lines of foam along the shores of New England. He gained the confidence of the patriot party, of which he was the natural leader. His influence became predominant. He was the peer of the two Adamses, and touched hands right and left with the foremost men of all the colonies.

It surprises us to note that at this time James Otis devoted a considerable section of his time to scholastic and literary pursuits. He was a student not only of men and affairs but of books. Now it was that the influence of his Harvard education was seen in both his studies and his works. We are surprised to find him engaged in the composition of a text-book which is still extant, and, however obsolete, by no means devoid of merits. The work was clearly a result left on his mind from his student days.

He composed and, in the year 1760, published, by the house of B. Mecom in Boston, a 72 page brochure entitled "The Rudiments of Latin Prosody with a Dissertation on Letters and the Principles of Harmony in Poetic and Prosaic Composition, collected from some of the best Writers."

The work is primarily a text in Latin Prosody in which the author thought himself to improve on the existing treatises on that subject. The afterpart of the pamphlet is devoted to a curious examination of the qualities of the letters of the Greek and Roman alphabets.

In this he attempts to teach the distinction between quantity and accent in the Greek language, but more particularly to describe the position and physiological action of the organs of speech in producing the elementary sounds in the languages referred to. The author declares his conviction that the growth of science had been seriously impeded by the inattention of people to the correct utterance of elementary sounds. He also points out the great abuses in the prevailing methods and declares that these abuses have so impeded the work of education "that many have remained children all their days."

Having written and published his work on Latin prosody, Mr. Otis next produced a similar work on the prosody of Greek. This, however, he did not publish, and he is said to have destroyed the manuscript at the time of burning his correspondence near the end of his life.

A conversation of James Otis is narrated by Francis Bowen, in Jared Sparks's "American Biography" in which the orator is represented, in speaking of the bad literary taste prevalent among the boys of the time, as saying, "These lads are very fond of talking about poetry and repeating passages of it. The poets they quote I know nothing of; but do you take care, James, [Otis was addressing James Perkins, Esq., of Boston] that you don't give in to this folly. If you want to read poetry, read Shakespeare, Milton, Dryden and Pope and throw all the rest into the fire; these are all that are worth reading." In this brief comment the severity of Otis's literary taste is indicated and also something of the rather abrupt and dogmatic character of his mind. His criticism, though true, can hardly be said to be judicious.

In order to understand the part which James Otis played in the great work of revolution and independence it is now necessary to note with care the conditions into which he was cast and with which he was environed at that period of his life when the man-fire flames highest and the audacity of the soul bounds furthest into the arena of danger.

Every man is the joint product of himself and his environment. His life is the resultant of the two forces by which he is held and balanced. At the time when James Otis reached his thirty-fifth year a condition had supervened in the American colonies which reacted upon his passionate and Patriotic nature so powerfully as to bring into full play all of his faculties and to direct the whole force of his nature against the tyrannical method of the mother country.

Let us look for a moment at the course of events which had preceded and which succeeded the crisis in James Otis's life, and made him the born leader of his countrymen in their first conflict for independence.

Great Britain had aforetime permitted the American colonists to plant themselves where, when, and as they would. Almost every colonial settlement had been an adventure. The emigrants from the other side of the Atlantic had been squeezed out by the hard discipline of church and state. In America they settled as they might.

"And England didn't look to know or care."

In the language of one of the bards of this age,

"That is England's awful way of doing business."

She permitted her persecuted children to brave the intolerable ocean in leaking ships, to reach the new world if they could, and survive if they might.

Notwithstanding this hard strain on the sentiment of the Pilgrims, the Cavaliers, and the Hugenots, they remained loyal to the mother country. They built their little states in the wilderness and were proud to christen their towns and villages with the cherished names of the home places in England. They defended themselves as well as they could against the inhospitality of nature, the neglect of the mother country, and the cruelty of savage races.

It was only when they grew and multiplied and flourished that our little seashore republics attracted the attention of the mother land and suggested to the ministers of the crown the possibility of plucking something from the new states which had now demonstrated their ability to exist and to yield an increase.

Meanwhile, for six generations, the colonists had developed their own social affairs and managed their own civil affairs according to the exegencies of the case and the principles of democracy. Their methods of government were necessarily republican.

The military necessities which were ever at the door had taught our fathers the availability of arms as the final argument in the debate with wrong. The conflicts with the Indians and the experiences of the French and Indian war had shown that the Americans were able to hold their own in battle.

Under these conditions there was a natural growth of public opinion in the colonies tending to independence of action, and to indignant protest against foreign dictation. In the sixth decade of the eighteenth century many of the leading young men of America talked and wrote of independence as a thing desirable and possible.

In 1755, when James Otis was thirty years of age, his young friend, John Adams, sitting one day in his school house in Connecticut, wrote this in his diary: "In another century all Europe will not be able to subdue us. The only way to keep us from setting up for ourselves is to disunite us."

We thus note natural conditions as tending to produce a rebellion of the American colonies; also the inherited disposition of the colonists under the discipline of their times; also the growth of public opinion among the leading spirits--to which we must add the character of the reigning king and of the ministers to whom he entrusted his government as the general conditions antecedent to the revolutionary movement of our fathers.

But there were more immediate and forceful causes which operated to the same end. Among these should be mentioned as a prevailing influence the right of arbitrary government claimed by Great Britain and at length resisted by the colonists. The right of arbitrarily controlling the American states was shown in a number of specific acts which we must here discuss.

The first of these was the old Navigation Act of 1651. The measure adopted by the government of Cromwell had never been strenuously enforced. It was the peculiarity of all the early legislation of Great Britain relative to the colonies that it was either misdirected or permitted to lapse by disuse.

The colonies thus literally grew, with little home direction. After the navigation act had been nominally in force for eighty-two years it was revived and supplemented by another measure known as the Importation Act.

This statute, dating from the year 1733, was intended to be an actual device for controlling the commercial relations with the colonies. By the terms of the Act heavy duties were laid on all the sugar, molasses, and rum which should be imported into the colonies. The customs were exorbitant and were from the first evaded as far as possible by the American merchants.

This may be regarded as the first actual breach of justice on the one side and good faith on the other, as between the home government and the American dependencies of Great Britain.

The reader will note that the question at issue was from the first commercial. It was a question of taking something from the colonists and of giving no equivalent, either in value or political rights. Had the American colonists been willing to be taxed and searched without an equivalent, then would there have been no revolution.

It will be noted from the nature of the question that the issue, since it was a matter of the merchants, was also a matter of the cities. For the merchant and the city go together. With the country folk of the pre-revolutionary era, the faultfinding and dispute related always to political questions proper--to questions of rights as between the king and his subjects; to questions of institutional forms, the best method of governing, etc.

All of these matters, however, could have been easily adjusted, and if there were an "if" in history they would have been adjusted without revolution and without independence. The commercial question, however, involving money rights, and implying the privilege and power of the Mother Country to take from the Colonists their property, however small the amount, could but engender resistance, and if the claim were not relinquished could but lead to war and disruption.

The neglected growth of the Colonies had in the meantime established in the seaboard towns of America, usages and customs which were repugnant to British notions of regular and orderly government. The commercial life had taken a form of its own.

The Americans had built ships and warehouses. They had engaged in commerce as they would. They had made their trade as free as possible. They had ignored the old Navigation Act, and when the Importation Act was passed, it confronted a condition in America.

It applied to a state of affairs that already existed.

The American ship, trading with the West Indies and bringing back to Boston a cargo of molasses or rum, was met at custom house with an exorbitant requisition. The officer acting under the Importation Act, virtually said, "Stand and deliver."

If it were a British ship the resistance to the duty would be offered by the land merchants rather than by the sea traders; for the merchants did not desire that the cost of the merchandise to themselves and their customers should be doubled without some equivalent advantage. No equivalent advantage was either visible or invisible. What, therefore, should they do but first evade and then openly resist?

There was an epoch of evasion. This covered a period of about seventeen years, extending from 1733 to 1750. In the latter year an act was passed by Parliament forbidding the erection of iron works in America. The manufacture of steel was especially interdicted. The measure which was in reality directed against shipbuilding included a provision which forbade the felling of pines outside of enclosures. It was thus sought by indirection to prevent the creation of a merchant marine by the American Colonists and to limit their commerce to British ships. This measure like the Importation Act was also ignored and resisted. For eleven years the Americans persisted in their usual course, making iron, cutting pine timber and building ships, importing molasses and rum, evading the duties, and thus getting themselves into the category of smugglers.

It was this precise condition of affairs which led to a still more stringent measure on the part of the home government. It was determined in Parliament to put an end to the evasion and resistance of the American merchants and importers with respect to the existing laws. The customs should be collected. It was deemed best, however, that the new measure should issue from the judiciary.

An appeal was made to the Court of Exchequer in England for the granting of search warrants to be issued in America by the king's officers for the purpose of ferreting out contraband goods. These warrants granted by the Court of Exchequer were the Writs of Assistance, the name of which appears so frequently and with so much odium in the colonial history of the times. These writs were granted by the court under pressure of the ministry in the year 1760.

The Writs of Assistance were directed to the officers of the customs in America. But any officer could arm one of his subordinates, or indeed any other person whom he should designate, with one of the writs, and the person so appointed might act in the name of the king's officer.

The thing to be done was the examination of any place and all places where contraband goods might be supposed to be lodged. Whether there were evidence or no evidence, the case was the same. The document was a writ of arbitrary search.

Any house, public or private, might be entered at any time; any closet or any cellar might be opened. Neither the bridal chamber nor the room of the dead was sacred on the approach of any petty customs constable or deputy in whose hands a Writ of Assistance had been placed. The antecedent proceedings required no affidavit or any other legal formality. The object was to lay bare the whole privacy of a people on sheer suspicion of smuggling.

It could hardly be supposed that our fathers would tamely submit to such an odious and despotic procedure. To have done so would have been to subscribe to a statute for their own enslavement. Nor may we pass from the consideration of these writs and the resistance offered thereto by the patriots of all our colonies without noticing the un-English character of these laws.

Of a certainty Englishmen in whatever continent or island of this world would never tolerate such a tyrannical interference with their rights. This was demonstrated not only in America, but in England also.

The issuance in England of just such illegal and arbitrary warrants was one of the causes that led to the tremendous agitation headed by John Wilkes. The excitement in that controversy grew, and notwithstanding the repeated arrests of Wilkes and his expulsions from Parliament, his reelection was repeated as often, and his following increased until not only the ministry but the throne itself was shaken by the cry of "Wilkes and Liberty." Nor did this well-timed ebullition of human rights subside until the arbitrary warrants were annulled by a decision of the King's Bench.

It was the trial of this issue in America that brought on the Revolution. It was a great cause that had to be pleaded, and the occasion and the city and the man, were as great as the cause. The parties to it were clearly defined, and were set in sharp antagonism.

On the one side were the king's officers in the province, headed by the governor. This following included the officers of the customs in particular. It also included the not inconsiderable class of American respectabilities who were feeble in American sentiments, and who belonged by nature and affiliation to the established order. These were the loyalists, destined to be designated as Tories, and to become the bete noire of patriotism.

On the other side was a whole phalanx of the common people--a phalanx bounded on the popular side by the outskirt of society and on the high-up side by the intellectual and philosophical patriots who were as pronounced as any for the cause of their country, and with better reason than the reason of the many.

The officers of the province elected by the home folks were all patriots, but the appointed officers of the crown were quite unanimous for the prerogative of the crown, holding severe measures should be taken with the resisting colonists, and in particular that the Writs of Assistance were good law and correct policy.

We should here note the particular play of the personal forces in the year 1760. There were two notable deaths--the one notable in Massachusetts and the other in the world. The first was that of Chief Justice Stephen Sewall of Massachusetts, and the other was that of His Majesty George II, the

"Snuffy old drone from the German hive,"

as he is described by the "Autocrat of the Breakfast Table." The first was succeeded in office by Thomas Hutchinson, Lieutenant-Governor of the province under Sir Fraucis Bernard, who was appointed governor in this notable year 1760 as the successor of Thomas Pownall, who had succeeded Governor William Shirley.

Hutchinson--to use the adjective which John Adams was wont to apply to himself and other patriots to the manner born--was a Massachusettensian. He had sympathized with the people, but he now turned against them. Before Judge Sewall went away it was said and believed that Governor Shirley had promised the place of Chief Justice, when the same should be vacant, to no other than Colonel James Otis of Barnstable, father of the subject of this sketch.

But Governor Bernard, Shirley's second successor in office, took another view of the matter and appointed Lieutenant-Governor Hutchinson to the high office of Chief Justice.

It was the belief and allegation of the King's party that this appointment and this disappointment--the first of Hutchinson and the second of Colonel Otis-- bore heavily on all the Otises, and indeed converted them from royalism to patriotism.

Chief Justice Hutchinson himself is on record to this effect. In his "History of Massachusetts," speaking of his own appointment to the judicial office, he says:

"The expected opposition ensued. Both gentlemen (that is, Colonel Otis and James Otis, Jr.) had been friends to the government. From this time they were at the head of every measure in opposition, not merely in those points which concerned the Governor in his administration, but in such as concerned the authority of Parliament; the opposition to which first began in this colony, and was moved and conducted by one of them, both in the Assembly and the town of Boston. From so small a spark, a great fire seems to have been kindled."

The statement of a partisan, especially if he be a beneficiary, must be taken with the usual allowance of salt.

It may be that the patriotic trend of the Otises was intensified a little by a personal pique in the matter referred to. But that either father or son was transferred from the king's party to the people's party by the failure of Colonel Otis to be appointed Chief Justice is not to be believed. Other stories are to be dismissed in the same manner.

One slander prevalent about the Custom House ran to the effect that James Otis had declared that he would set the province on fire even if he had to perish in the flames. The art of political lying was known even among our fathers.

Such was the situation of affairs when the sycophants of the foreign government in Boston undertook to enforce the Writs of Assistance. They soon found that they needed more assistance to do it. The banded merchants, and the patriots generally, said that the acts were illegal, and that they would not submit to the officers. The governor and his subordinates and the custom-house retinue in particular, said that the writs were legal, and that they should be enforced. The matter came to a clash and a trial.

The case as made up presented this question: Shall the persons employed in enforcing the Acts of Trade have the power to invoke generally the assistance of all the executive officers of the colony?

This issue was, in February of 1761, taken into court in the old Town House, afterwards the old State House, of Boston. There were sitting the five Judges of the Superior Court of the province. Chief Justice Hutchinson, still holding the office of Lieutenant-Governor, his membership in the Council, and his position of Judge of Probate, presided at the trial. Perhaps there was never in America an instance in which a high official so nearly fulfilled the part of "Pooh Bah."

The trial evoked an attendance of all who could be admitted, and of many more. The officers of the crown were out in full force, and resolute patriotism completed the crowd. John Adams was one of the spectators.

Another element in the dramatic situation was the fact that James Otis had, in the meantime, received the appointment to the crown office of Advocate General, to which an ample salary was attached. In this relation it would be his especial duty to support the petition of the custom-house officers in upholding the Writs of Assistance and in constraining the executive officers of the province to support them in doing so.

This contingency brought out the mettle of the man. When the revenue officers came to him with the request that he defend their case, he at once resigned his office, and this being known the merchants immediately sought his services as counsel to uphold their protest against the Writs. For his assistant they selected Mr. Oxenbridge Thatcher.

Otis accepted the invitation without a fee. His action involved the loss of his official position as well as his means of living.

It chanced at this time that his old law preceptor, Jeremiah Gridley, was selected as King's Attorney, and it fell to his lot to take the place which Otis would not accept. Thus master and pupil were brought face to face at the bar in the hottest legal encounter which preceded our rupture with the mother country.

The trial that ensued has been described by John Adams, an eye witness of the whole proceedings. He gives in his works a description of the conduct of the case as it was presented for and against the crown, and also notes of Otis's argument.

After the pleas were presented and other preliminary matters arranged, Mr. Gridley addressed the court in support of the government's position. He defended the petition of the custom-house officials as both legal and just. Two statutes of the time of Charles II, empowering the court of Exchequer to issue writs such as those which were now denied, were adduced. He then cited the statute of the sixth year of Queen Anne, which continued to inforce the processes which had been authorized in the twelfth and fourteenth years of the reign of Charles.

Still more to the point were the statutes of the seventh and eighth years of William III, which authorized the collection of revenue "in the British plantations" by officers who might search both public and private houses to find goods that had evaded the duty. These statutes Mr. Gridley claimed as a warrant for the like usage in America.

In answer to Gridley, Oxenbridge Thatcher,[1] himself a lawyer of no mean abilities, spoke for the counter petitioners. His plea was a strong confutation of Gridley's arguments. After this brief address Mr. Otis rose to continue the plea for the people.

Of the speech which followed we have no complete record or wholly satisfactory summary. It is to John Adams, and to the notes which he made on the occasion, that we must look for our opinion of what was, if we mistake not, the greatest and most effective oration delivered in the American colonies before the Revolution.

Such was the accepted belief of those who heard Otis, and witnessed the effect of his tremendous oratory.

Making all allowance for exaggeration, it seems to have been one of those inspired appeals by which History and Providence at critical epochs make themselves known to mankind. John Adams, then twenty-five years of age, passing from his notes of Thatcher's speech, says of the greater actor:

"But Otis was a flame of fire; with a promptitude of classical allusions, a depth of research, a rapid summary of historical events and dates, a profusion of legal authorities, a prophetic glance of his eyes into futurity, and a rapid torrent of impetuous eloquence, he hurried away all before him. American Independence was then and there born. The seeds of patriots and heroes, to defend the Non sine diis animosus infans, to defend the vigorous youth, were then and there sown. Every man of an immense crowded audience appeared to me to go away, as I did, ready to take arms against Writs of Assistance. Then and there was the first scene of the first act of opposition to the arbitrary claims of Great Britain. Then and there the child Independence was born. In fifteen years, that is in 1776, he grew up to manhood, and declared himself free."

We may allow a little for the enthusiasm of a young patriot such as Adams, but there can be no doubt that his unmeasured eulogy was well deserved. Such was the description of Otis's speech.

As to the speech itself we have only a second-hand and inadequate report. Minot, in his "History of Massachusetts," presents what purports to be a tolerably full outline of the great address.

Mr. Otis spoke for five hours, during which time with his rather rapid utterance he would perhaps deliver an oration of 30,000 words. Minot's report appears to have been derived from Adams' notes done into full form by an unknown writer, who probably put in here and there some rather florid paragraphs of his own. At a subsequent period, Adams took up the subject and corrected Minot's report, giving the revised address to William Tudor, who used the same in his biography of James Otis. From these sources we are able to present a fair abstract of what were the leading parts of Otis's speech. In the beginning he said:

"May it please your Honors:

"I was desired by one of the court to look into the books, and consider the question now before them concerning Writs of Assistance. I have accordingly considered it, and now appear, not only in obedience to your order, but likewise in behalf of the inhabitants of this town, who have present another petition, and out of regard to the liberties of the subject. And I take this liberty to declare, that, whether under a fee or not (for in such a cause as this I despise a fee), I will to my dying day oppose, with all the powers and faculties God has given me, all such instruments of slavery on the one hand, and villainy on the other, as this Writ of Assistance is.

"It appears to me the worst instrument of arbitrary power, the most destructive of English liberty and the fundamental principles of law, that was ever found in an English law-book. I must, therefore, beg your Honors' patience and attention to the whole range of an argument, that may, perhaps, appear uncommon in many things, as well as to points of learning that are more remote and unusual, that the whole tendency of my design may the more easily be perceived, the conclusions better descend, and the force of them be better felt.

"I shall not think much of my pains in this case, as I engaged in it from principle. I was solicited to argue this case as advocate-general; and because I would not, I have been charged with desertion from my office. To this charge I can give a very sufficient answer. I renounced that office, and I argue this case, from the same principle; and I argue it with the greater pleasure, as it is in favor of British liberty, at a time when we hear the greatest monarch upon earth declaring from his throne, that he glories in the name of Briton, and that the privileges of his people are dearer to him than the most valuable prerogatives of his crown; and it is in opposition to a kind of power, the exercise of which, in former periods of English history, cost one king of England his head, and another his throne.

"I have taken more pains in this case than I ever will take again, although my engaging in this and another popular case has raised much resentment. But I think I can sincerely declare, that I cheerfully submit myself to every odious name for conscience' sake; and from my soul I despise all those whose guilt, malice or folly, has made them my foes.

"Let the consequences be what they will, I am determined to proceed. The only principles of public conduct, that are worthy of a gentleman or a man, are to sacrifice estate, ease, health and applause, and even life, to the sacred calls of his country.

"These manly sentiments, in private life, make the good citizen; in public life, the patriot and the hero. I do not say that, when brought to the test, I shall be invincible. I pray God I may never be brought to the melancholy trial; but if ever I should, it will then be known how far I can reduce to practice principles which I know to be founded in truth. In the meantime, I will proceed to the subject of this writ."

After this introductory part we are obliged to fall back on the summary given by Mr. Adams. According to his report, Otis in the next place went into fundamentals and discussed the rights of man in a state of nature. In this part, the argument ran in an analagous vein to that of Rousseau in the Contrat Social that is, man in the first place is a sovereign subject only to the higher laws revealed in his own conscience. In this state he has a right to life, to liberty, to property.

Here the speaker fell into the manner of Jefferson in the opening paragraphs of the Declaration. It is to be noted that Otis presented the truth absolutely; he including negroes in the common humanity to whom inalienable rights belong.

Mr. Otis next took up the social compact, and showed that society is the individual enlarged and generalized. This brought him to the question before the court; for the conflict now on was a struggle of society, endowed with inalienable rights, against arbitrary authority and its abusive exercise.

The abusive exercise was shown in the attempts to enforce the Acts of Trade. Of this kind was the old Navigation Act, and of like character was the Importation Act. It was to enforce these that the Writs of Assistance had been devised. Mr. Otis then continued:

"Your Honors will find, in the old books concerning the office of a justice of the peace, precedents of general warrants to search suspected houses. But, in more modern books, you will find only special warrants to search such and such houses, specially named, in which the complainant has before sworn, that he suspects his goods are concealed; and will find it adjudged, that special warrants only are legal. In the same manner, I rely in it, that the writ prayed for in this petition, being general, is illegal. It is a power that places the liberty of every man in the hands of every petty officer.

"I say, I admit that special Writs of Assistance, to search special places, may be granted to certain persons on oath; but I deny that the writ now prayed for can be granted; for I beg leave to make some observations on the writ itself, before I proceed to other acts of Parliament.

"In the first place, the writ is universal, being directed to 'all and singular justices, sheriffs, constables, and all other officers and subjects;' so that, in short, it is directed to every subject in the King's dominions. Every one, with this writ, may be a tyrant in a legal manner, and may control, imprison, or murder, any one within the realm.

"In the next place it is perpetual; there is no return. A man is accountable to no person for his doings. Every man may reign secure in his petty tyranny, and spread terror and desolation around him, until the trump of the archangel shall excite different emotions in his soul.

"In the third place, a person with this writ, in the daytime, may enter all houses, shops, etc., at will, and command all to assist him.

"Fourthly, by this writ, not only deputies, etc., but even their menial servants, are allowed to lord it over us. What is this but to have the curse of Canaan with a witness on us? To be the servant of servants, the most despicable of God's creation?

"Now, one of the most essential branches of English liberty is the freedom of one's house. A man's house is his castle; and whilst he is quiet, he is as well guarded as a prince in his castle. This writ, if it should be declared legal, would totally annihilate this privilege. Custom-house officers may enter our houses when they please; we are commanded to permit their entry. Their menial servants may enter, may break locks, bars, and every thing in their way; and whether they break through malice or revenge, no man, no court, can inquire. Bare suspicion, without oath, is sufficient.

"This wanton exercise of this power is not a chimerical suggestion of a heated brain. I will mention some facts. Mr. Pew had one of these writs, and, when Mr. Ware succeeded him, he endorsed this writ over to Mr. Ware; so that these writs are negotiable from one officer to another; and so your Honors have no opportunity of judging the persons to whom this vast power is delegated. Another instance is this:

"Mr. Justice Walley had called this same Mr. Ware before him, by a constable, to answer for a breach of the Sabbath-day acts, or that of profane swearing. As soon as he had finished, Mr. Ware asked him if he had done. He replied, 'Yes.' 'Well, then,' said Mr. Ware, 'I will show you a little of my power. I command you to permit me to search your house for uncustomed goods;' and went on to search the house from the garret to the cellar; and then served the constable in the same manner.

"But to show another absurdity in this writ, if it be established, I insist upon it, every person, by the 14th of Charles the Second, has this power, as well as the custom-house officers. The words are, 'It shall be lawful for any person, or persons, authorized,' etc. What a scene does this open. Every man prompted by revenge, ill-humor, or wantonness, to inspect the inside of his neighbor's house, may get a Writ of Assistance. Others will ask it from self-defence; one arbitrary exertion will provoke another, until society be involved in tumult and in blood."

This extract may serve to show the Demosthenic power of James Otis as an orator. We cannot within our limits present many additional paragraphs from his great plea in the cause of his countrymen.

To the next division of his argument he confuted the position taken by Gridley with respect to the alleged legal precedents for the Writs of Assistance. He showed that the writs were wholly different from those provided for in the time of Charles II. Even if they had not been so, the epoch and the manner of King Charles had passed away. Neither could the Writs be justified by inferences and constructions deduced from any previous statutes of Parliament.

Besides, such odious Writs could never be enforced. They could never be enforced in the City of the Pilgrims. If the King of England should himself encamp with twenty thousand soldiers on the Common of Boston, he could not enforce such laws. He assailed the sugar tax with unmeasured invective. And over and above all, this despotic legislation was in direct conflict with the Charter of Massachusetts.

Here the orator broke forth in his most impassioned strain declaring that the British King, the British Parliament and the British nation, were all guilty of ingratitude and oppression in attempting to impose tyrannical enactment on the people of America. Thus he concluded his argument appeal.

Those who heard the oration were convulsed with excitement. The King's party was enraged. The patriots were inspired and defiant. It was in every respect a critical and a historic hour.

What would the court do with the case? The action of that body was obscure and double. There seems to have been a disposition of the Associate Judges to decide for the counter-petitioners; but Chief Justice Hutchinson induced them to assent to his policy of withholding a decision. He accordingly announced that the court would decide the case at the ensuing session. He then wrote to the home government, and the records show that the decision was rendered for the petitioners. That is, for the Custom House officials, and in favor of the Writs.

The Chief Justice is also on record to the effect that he continued to issue the Writs; but if so, no officer of the king ever dared to present one of them in Boston! The famous (and infamous) Writs of Assistance were as dead as the mummies of Egypt.

It is from this point of view that the character and work of James Otis appear to the greatest historical advantage. There can be no doubt that his was the living voice which called to resistance, first Boston, then Massachusetts, then New England and then the world! For ultimately the world heard the sound thereof and was glad. The American Colonies resisted, and at length won their independence. The sparks fell in France, and the jets of flame ran together in a conflagration the light of which was seen over Europe, and if over Europe, then over the world. The Pre-revolutionist had cried out and mankind heard him. Resistance to tyranny became obedience to God.

We shall here sketch rapidly and briefly the unsteady way and unfortunate decline of James Otis down to the time of the eclipse of his intellect and his tragic death.

Three months after he had, according to John Adams; "breathed into the nation the breath of life," he was chosen to represent Boston in the legislature of the Commonwealth. All of his colleagues were patriots. Boston was in that mood.

There runs a story that when he was entering upon his duties he was counselled by a friend to curb his impetuosity and to gain leadership by the mastery of self--advice most salutary to one of his temperament. But it was much like advising General Putnam to be calm at Bunker Hill! Otis promised, however, that if his friends would warn him when his temperature was rising, he would command himself.

It is also narrated that his friends did attempt to pluck him by the coat, but he turned upon them demanding to know if he was a school boy to be called down!

At this time the relations between Governor Bernard and the Legislature were greatly strained. Otis rather increased the tension. A question arose about a financial measure whereby gold was to be exported and silver money retained as the currency of the colony--the former at less than its nominal value--in a manner to juggle the people into paying their obligations twice over. The argument became hot and the Council taking the side of the administration was opposed by the legislative assembly.

Chief Justice Hutchinson and James Otis got into a controversy which was bitter enough, and which may be illustrated with the following letter which James Otis addressed to the printer of a newspaper:

"Perhaps I should not have troubled you or the public with any thoughts of mine, had not his Honor the Lieutenant-Governor condescended to give me a personal challenge. This is an honor that I never had vanity enough to aspire after, and I shall ever respect Mr. Hutchinson for it so long as I live, as he certainly consulted my reputation more than his own when he bestowed it. A general officer in the army would be thought very condescending to accept, much more to give, a challenge to a subaltern. The honor of entering the lists with a gentleman so much one's superior in one view is certainly tempting; it is at least possible that his Honor may lose much; but from those who have and desire but little, but little can possibly be taken away.

"I am your humble servant, "JAMES OTIS, JR."

This controversy continued for some time, and it is thought that to it must be attributed much of the animosity displayed by the Chief Justice towards Otis in the "History of Massachusetts Bay."

Mr. Otis continued his aggressive policy in the session of the assembly held in 1762. It was at this session that the government in the hope of getting a sum of money adopted the ruse of creating an alarm relative to a French invasion of Newfoundland. But the patriots would have none of it. They went so far as to say that if arbitrary government was to be established in America, it made no difference whether the Americans should have King Stork or King Log. To this effect ran a resolution offered by James Otis:

"No necessity can be sufficient to justify a House of Representatives in giving up such a privilege; for it would be of little consequence to the people, whether they were subject to George or Louis, the King of Great Britain or the French King; if both were arbitrary, as both would be, if both could levy taxes without Parliament."

It is said that when this resolution was offered a loyalist member cried out in the Virginian manner, "Treason, treason." It was in this way that Mr. Otis gained the undying enmity of the King's party in America.

It was in the period following his legislative service that James Otis prepared his powerful pamphlet entitled "A Vindication of the Conduct of the House of Representatives of the Province of the Massachusetts Bay." In this work he traverses and justifies the course pursued by the patriot legislature during the sessions of his attendance.

Great was the joy of the American Colonies at the conclusion of the French and Indian War. The Treaty of Paris in February of 1763 conceded Canada to Great Britain and insured the predominance of English institutions in the New World.

The animosities of the Americans towards the mother country rapidly subsided. Meetings were held in the principal towns to ratify the peace. At the jubilee in Boston, James Otis presided.

He made on the occasion one of his notable addresses. He referred with enthusiasm to the "expulsion of the heathen"-- meaning the French, and then expressed sentiments of strong affection for Great Britain and appreciation of the filial relations of the American Colonies to her.

In these utterances Otis reflected the sentiment of the Bostonians and of the whole people. The General Assembly of Massachusetts took up the theme and passed resolutions of gratitude and loyalty. At this particular juncture the Americans did not anticipate what was soon to follow.

The English Ministry was already preparing a scheme for the raising of revenue in America: The question of the right of taxation suddenly obtruded itself. The Americans claimed the right as Englishmen to tax themselves. The English ministers replied that Parliament, and not the Colonial Assemblies, was the proper body to vote taxes in any and all parts of the British Empire. The Americans replied that they were not represented in Parliament. Parliament replied that many of the towns, shires, and boroughs in England were not represented. If they were not represented, they ought to be, said the Americans;--and thus the case was made up.

By the beginning of 1764 it was known that the Ministers had determined to make a rigorous enforcement of the Sugar Act. Than this, nothing could be more odious to America.

In the spring of the year just named, the citizens of Boston held a great meeting to protest against the impending policy of the crown. As a member of the Assembly and as chairman of a committee Mr. Otis made a report which was ordered to be sent to the agent of the government along with the copy of Otis's recent pamphlet, "The Rights of the British Colonies asserted and proved."

At this time Lieutenant-Governor Hutchinson was about to become the representative of the Colony in its contention with the crown and for some reason, not very apparent, Mr. Otis favored his appointment. Governor Bernard, however, opposed the measure, and Hutchinson declined the appointment. Otis's course was censured by the patriots and his popularity was for the while impaired. However, he took strong grounds against the Sugar Act, and soon afterward still more strenuously opposed the Stamp Act.

He regained the impaired confidence of the people and at the close of the session of the Assembly he was appointed chairman of a committee to correspond with the other Colonies, and thus to promote the common interest of all. This, after the intercolonial conference which Franklin had promoted, was perhaps the first step towards the creation of the Continental Congress. Mr. Otis's letter to the provincial agent went to England, though it was sent in the name of the Lower House only. In this document the writer said:

"Granting the time may come, which we hope is far off, when the British Parliament shall think fit to oblige the North Americans, not only to maintain civil government among themselves, for this they have already done, but to support an army to protect them, can it be possible, that the duties to be imposed and the taxes to be levied shall be assessed without the voice or consent of one American in Parliament? If we are not represented, we are slaves."

This document was one of the few American papers which was read and criticized in the British Parliament. The merits of Mr. Otis's pamphlet were actually debated in the House of Lords by Lord Littleton and Lord Mansfield.

The latter in the course of his remarks said:

"Otis is a man of consequence among the people there. They have chosen him for one of their deputies at the Congress, and general meeting from the respective governments. It is said the man is mad. What then? One madman often makes many. Massaniello was mad, nobody doubts; yet for all that, he overturned the government of Naples. Madness is catching in all popular assemblies, and upon all popular matters. The book is full of wildness. I never read it till a few days ago, for I seldom look into such things."

It was in the course of this pamphlet that the Mr. Otis spoke so strongly on taxation and representation. "The very act of taxing," said he, "exercised over those who are not represented, appears to me to be depriving them of one of their most essential rights; and, if continued seems to be, in effect, an entire disfranchisement of every civil right. For what one civil right is worth a rush, after a man's property is subject to be taken from him at pleasure, without his consent?"[2]

In this was the germ of the stern resistance offered by the Americans to the Stamp Act. No man in the colonies did so much to confute the principles on which the Stamp Act rested as did James Otis.

When the General Assembly of Massachusetts met in May of 1765, Governor Bernard urged in his address the duty of submission to Parliament as to the "conservators of liberty." It was this recommendation which being referred to a Committee, of which Otis was a member, led to the adoption of a resolution for the holding of a Colonial Congress in New York.

Nine colonies accepted the invitation of Massachusetts, and James Otis headed the delegation of three members chosen to represent the mother colony in that prophetic body.

The story of the contest of the Americans with the home government on the subject of the Stamp Act is well known. The controversy resulted on the 18th of March, 1766, in the repeal of the Act by Parliament. But the repeal was accompanied with a salvo to British obduracy in the form of a declaration that Parliament had "the right to bind the colonies in all cases whatsoever."

Notwithstanding this hateful addendum, the repeal of the Act was received in America with the greatest joy. During the excitement antecedent to the repeal, mobs had surged through the streets of Boston, building bonfires and burning effigies of officers and other adherents of the king's party. In one of these ebullitions, the house of Lieutenant-Governor Hutchinson was attacked and pillaged. The better people had nothing to do with it. Many were arrested and imprisoned.

Governor Bernard was so much alarmed that he declared himself to be a governor only in name. The partisans of the crown started a story that James Otis was the instigator of the riots. There is a hint to this effect in Hutchinson's "History of Massachusetts Bay." But it is evident that the charge was unfounded--except in this, that in times of public excitement the utterances of orators are frequently wrested from their purpose by the ignorant and made to do service in the cause of anarchy.

Meanwhile on the first of November, Mr. Otis returned from the Congress in New York, laid a copy of the proceedings before the Assembly, and was formally thanked for his services.

During the Stamp Act year, Mr. Otis found time to compose two pamphlets setting forth his views on the great questions of the day. There had recently appeared a letter written by a Halifax gentleman and addressed to a Rhode Island friend. The latter personage was unknown; the former was ascertained to be a certain Mr. Howard. The so-called "Letter" was written with much ability and in a bitter spirit.

To this Otis replied with great asperity, and with his power of invective untrammeled. He called his pamphlet "A Vindication of the British Colonies against the Aspersions of the Halifax Gentleman, in his Letter to a Rhode Island Friend." A single passage from the work may serve to show the cogency of the writer's style and especially his anticipation of the doctrines of the Declaration of Independence.

"Is the gentleman," said he, "a British-born subject and a lawyer, and ignorant that charters from the crown have usually been given for enlarging the liberties and privileges of the grantees, not for limiting them, much less for curtailing those essential rights, which all his Majesty's subjects are entitled to, by the laws of God and nature, as well as by the common law and by the constitution of their country?

"The gentleman's positions and principles, if true, would afford a curious train of consequences. Life, liberty, and property are, by the law of nature, as well as by the common law, secured to the happy inhabitants of South Britain, and constitute their primary, civil, or political, rights."

The other pamphlet bearing date of September 4, 1765, was entitled "Considerations on Behalf of the Colonists, in a Letter to a Noble Lord." In this the writer discusses the question of Taxation and in particular the specious claim of the British Ministry that the home government might justly tax the colonists to defray the expenses of the French and Indian War.

In answer to this Otis says, in a manner worthy of an American patriot in the year 1898, "The national debt is confessed on all hands to be a terrible evil, and may in time ruin the state. But it should be remembered, that the colonies never occasioned its increase, nor ever reaped any of the sweet fruits of involving the finest kingdom in the world in the sad calamity of an enormous, overgrown mortgage to state and stock-jobbers."

The period here under consideration was that in which the Stamp Act was nominally in force. The law required all legal business to be done on stamped paper. Therefore no legal business was done.

Hutchinson in his History says: "No wills were proved, no administrations granted, no deeds nor bonds executed." Of course matters could not go on in this manner forever. Governor Bernard was induced to call the legislature together. When that body convened an answer to the Governor's previous message was adopted by the House, and the answer was the work of James Otis. An extract will show the temper of the people at that juncture:

"The courts of justice must be open, open immediately, and the law, the great rule of right, in every county in the province, executed. The stopping the courts of justice is a grievance which this House must inquire into. Justice must be fully administered through the province, by which the shocking effects which your Excellency apprehended from the people's non-compliance with the Stamp Act will be prevented."

Meanwhile the public agitation continued; the newspapers teemed with controversy. The administration was firm, but patriotism was rampant. The party of the people adopted the policy of embarrassing the government as much as possible. Then came the news of the repeal of the act, and the jubilation of the people to which we have already referred came after.

When the legislature met in May of 1767, James Otis was chosen speaker; but his election was vetoed by the Governor. The House was obliged to submit, which it did in sullen temper, and then chose Thomas Cushing for its presiding officer. The other elections indicated the patriotic purpose of the House.

There was almost a deadlock between the legislative and executive departments. Governor Bernard addressed the representatives in a supercilious and dogmatic manner, which they for their part resented with scant courtesy.

On one occasion they said (the language being Otis's) in a concluding paragraph: "With regard to the rest of your Excellency's speech, we are sorry we are constrained to observe, that the general air and style of it savor much more of an act of free grace and pardon, than of a parliamentary address to the two Houses of Assembly; and we most sincerely wish your Excellency had been pleased to reserve it, if needful, for a proclamation."

The state papers on affairs--at least that portion of them emanating from the legislative department--were, up to the year 1769, nearly all prepared by Mr. Otis; but it was generally necessary to tone down the first drafts of his work. For this duty the speaker (Thomas Cushing) and Samuel Adams were generally selected. It was reckoned necessary to put the damper on the fire!

The popular tendency at this time was illustrated in a proposition made by Mr. Otis to open the gallery of the House to such of the people as might wish to hear the debates.

Otis continued his correspondence, a great deal of which was official. His style and spirit suited the temper of the representatives, and they kept him occupied as chairman of a committee to answer messages from the

Government, and, indeed, messages from anybody who might assail the patriot party.

In the meantime the animosity between him and the Governor of the province waxed hot. The Governor constantly charged the patriot leader with being an incendiary, and the latter replied in a manner to convict Governor Bernard of despotic usages and a spirit hostile to American liberty.

The next measure adopted by Parliament inimical to the colonies was the act of 1767 imposing duties on glass, paper, painters' colors, and tea, and appointing a commission for the special purpose of collecting the revenues. The commissioners so appointed were to reside in the colonies.

This measure, hardly less odious than the Stamp Act, was strangely enough resisted with less vehemence. Several of the popular leaders were disposed to counsel moderation. Among these was Otis himself. But nearly all outside of the official circles were united against the new act. They formed associations and signed agreements not to use any of the articles on which the duty was imposed. This was equivalent to making the act of no effect.

In the legislative assembly of 1768, Mr. Otis was appointed with Samuel Adams to prepare an important paper on the state of public affairs. This they did by drawing up a petition which has been regarded as one of the ablest of its kind.

There is some controversy as to who actually wrote this famous paper, but it appears to have been done mostly by Mr. Otis, though the refining hand of Samuel Adams may be clearly seen in the style. The publication of the paper still further strained the relations between Governor Bernard and the representative branch.

Meanwhile, the news of the assembling of the Colonial Congress in New York had produced a sensation in England, and the petition of the Massachusetts legislature added to the temper of the ministry. In May of 1768, Bernard sent to the assembly a requisition that that body should rescind the resolution which they had passed for sending a circular letter to the other colonies.

To this Mr. Otis, acting for the assembly, prepared a reply which, while it was not less severe, was more respectful and concessive than were most of his communications. At the conclusion he says:

"We have now only to inform your Excellency, that this House have voted not to rescind, as required, the resolution of the last House; and that, upon a decision on the question, there were ninety-two nays and seventeen yeas."

In this manner the controversy dragged on through the years 1768-69, but in the summer of the former year an event occurred which roused the people to a high pitch of excitement. Some of the custom-house officers seized a vessel belonging to John Hancock. For this they were assailed by a mob which burned the boat of the collector of customs. The officers fled to the castle. It was for this business that a body of British soldiers was first sent to Boston.

On the 12th of September, 1768, a great meeting was held in Faneuil Hall, but the crowd was such as to make necessary and adjournment to Sewall's Meeting-house. James Otis was moderator of the meeting. The presence of British soldiers, evidently sent to Boston to enforce the decrees of an arbitrary government, was sufficient to bring into play all the elements of patriotism.

The British soldier's coat in the old town was of the same color as the scarf which the picador shakes in the face of the enraged animal! The effect in either case was the same.

At the meeting just mentioned, Mr. Otis presided and spoke. A report of what occurred was written (presumptively by some enemy of the patriots), and was sent as a report to the British ministry. In this Otis was charged with saying, "In case Great Britain is not disposed to redress our grievances after proper application, the people have nothing more to do, but to gird the sword on the thigh and shoulder the musket." Doubtless this report was a perversion of the truth.

Other meetings were held, and resolutions were the order of the day. On the 22nd of June, Faneuil Hall was again crowded. James Otis, Thomas Cushing, Samuel Adams, and John Hancock were selected as representatives to meet Committees of other towns in a convention. At this meeting it was voted that the people should arm themselves. The convention met with delegates present from nearly ninety towns. The movement against the ministerial scheme had already become revolutionary.

Meanwhile in 1768, the general assembly was unceremoniously prorogued by Governor Bernard, but in May of the following year, the body was re-convened. On the meeting day the building was surrounded with British troops.

Otis made an address, declaring that free legislation would be impossible in the presence of an armed soldiery. He moved the appointment of a committee to remonstrate with the Governor, and to request the withdrawal of the soldiers. To this the Governor replied evasively that he had not the authority to order the withdrawal of the military. Otis in answer reported that the Governor's reply was according to English law, more impossible than the thing which the Assembly had petitioned for.

The matter resulted in the adjournment of the body to meet at Cambridge, in the chapel of Harvard College. Assembled at that place the legislature was addressed by Otis with impassioned eloquence. The people as well as the legislators were gathered.

"The times are dark and trying," said the speaker. "We may soon be called on in turn to act or to suffer." "You," he continued, "should study and emulate the models of ancient patriotism. To you your country may one day look for support, and you should recollect that the noblest of all duties is to serve that country, and if necessary to devote your lives in her cause."

The House soon prepared a paper to be sent to the British Ministry denouncing the administration of Governor Bernard and protesting against the further presence of a British Soldiery in Boston. On the 27th of June, 1769, the representatives went further and prepared a petition, praying for the removal of Bernard from the government. This they might well do for the king had already recalled him!

The Governor went away in such odor as the breezes of the Old Bay have hardly yet dissipated. He went away, but in the fall added his compliments to the Americans by the publication of sundry letters in which they were traduced and vilified. To this James Otis and Samuel Adams, were appointed a committee to reply. They did so in a pamphlet entitled "An Appeal to the World, or a Vindication of the Town of Boston," etc.

It was in these tumultuous and honorable labors and excitements extending over a period of fully ten years that the intellect of James Otis became overstrained and, at length, warped from its purpose.

We may regard his rational career as ending with the year 1769. In September of this year it was noticed that he had become excitable, and that his natural eccentricity was accented at times to the extent of rendering his conduct irrational.

It was at this time that he published in the Boston "Gazette" what he called an advertisement, in which he placarded the four commissioners of customs, on the ground that they had assailed his character, declaring that they had formed a confederacy of villainy, and warning the officers of the crown to pay no attention to them.

On the evening of the following day, Mr. Otis went into a coffee-house where John Robinson, one of the commissioners whom he had lampooned, was sitting. On entering the room, Mr. Otis was attacked by Robinson who struck him with his cane. Otis struck back. There was a battle. Those who were present were Robinson's friends. The fight became a melee.

A young man named Gridley undertook to assist Otis, but was himself overpowered and pitched out of the house. Mr. Otis was seriously wounded in the head, and was taken to his house, bleeding and exhausted. The principle wound appeared to be inflicted with a sword; it was in the nature of a cut, and an empty scabbard was found on the floor of the room in which the altercation occurred.

On the morrow, Boston was aflame with excitement. Otis was seriously injured; in fact he never recovered from the effects of the assault. He brought suit against Robinson, and a jury gave a judgment of two thousand pounds damages against the defendant. The latter arose in court with a writing of open confession and apology, and hereupon the spirited and generous Otis refused to avail himself of the verdict.

Could he have thrown off the effects of the injury in like manner, his last years might have been a happier sequel to a useful and patriotic life.

During the sessions of the Assembly, in the years 1770 and 1771, James Otis retained his membership, but the mental disease which afflicted him began to grow worse, and he participated only at intervals (and eccentrically) in the business of legislation.

In May of 1770, a town meeting was held in Boston, and a resolution of thanks was passed to the distinguished representative for his services in the General Assembly. This was on the occasion of his retirement into the country, in the hope of regaining his health. At the close, the resolution declared:

"The town cannot but express their ardent wishes for the recovery of his (Mr. Otis's) health, and the continuance of those public services, that must long be remembered with gratitude, and distinguish his name among the Patriots of America."

From this time forth the usefulness of James Otis was virtually at an end. In the immortal drama on which the curtain was rising --the drama of Liberty and Independence--he was destined to take no part. The pre-revolutionist in eclipse must give place to the Revolutionist who was rising. John Adams came after, not wholly by his own ambition, but at the call of inexorable History, to take the part and place of the great Forerunner.

What must have been the thoughts and emotions of that Forerunner when the minute men of Massachusetts came firing and charging after the British soldiers in full retreat from Concord Bridge and Lexington? With what convulsion must his mind, in semi-darkness and ruin, have received the news of the still greater deed at Bunker Hill? History is silent as to what the broken Titan thought and said in those heroic days.

The patriot in dim eclipse became at times wholly rational, but with the least excitement his malady would return. In conversation something of his old brilliancy would return in flashes. For the rest, the chimes in that high soul no longer played the music of reason, but gave out only the discords of insanity. He was never reduced to serious delirium or to violent frenzy, but he was an insane man; and under this shadow he walked for the greater part of ten years, during which Independence was declared and the Revolution fought out to a victorious end.

It was in this period of decline and obscuration that James Otis witnessed through the gathering shadows the rise to distinction and fame of many of the patriots whom he had led in the first campaigns for liberty. John Adams and Hancock were now at the fore battling for independence. Among those who rose to eminence in the immortal eighth decade was Samuel Alleyne Otis, who in 1776 was elected a representative in the great Congress of the Revolution. James did not live to see his brother become speaker of the House, but he witnessed in 1780 his service as a member of the Constitutional Convention of Massachusetts. Afterward, in 1787, he was a commissioner to negotiate a settlement with the participants in Shay's Rebellion. With the organization of the new national government he became Secretary of the Senate of the United States, and served in that capacity until his death, April 22, 1814.

In 1781, Mr. Otis was taken by his friend, Colonel Samuel Osgood, to the home of the latter in Andover. There the enfeebled patriot passed the remainder of his life. He became very obese, and his nervous excitability to an extent subsided.

He was amiable and interesting to his friends. His health was in some measure restored, but his intellectual strength did not return. He thought of going back to Boston, and in one instance he accepted and conducted a case in the court of Common Pleas; but his manner was that of a paretic giant.

The favorable turn in Mr. Otis's condition was at length arrested by an attempt on his part to dine with Governor Hancock. At the dinner he was observed to become first sad and then to waver into mental occultation. He was taken by his brother, Hon. Samuel Alleyne Otis, to Andover. The event convinced the sufferer that the end of his life was not distant.

Strange, strange are the foregleams of the things to come! On one occasion he said to his sister, Mrs. Warren, "I hope when God Almighty in his Providence shall take me out of time into eternity, it will be by a flash of lightning!" The tradition goes that he frequently gave expression to this wish. Did the soul foresee the manner of its exit?

A marvelous and tragic end was indeed at hand. On the 23d of May, 1783, only a few months before the Briton left our shores never to return but by the courtesy of the Republic, a thundercloud, such as the season brings in New England, passed over Andover.

James Otis stood against the lintel of the door watching the commotion of the elements. There was a crash of thunder. The lightning, serpent-like, darted from heaven to earth and passed through the body of the patriot! Instantly he was dead.

There was no mark upon him; no contortion left its snarling twist on the placid features of him who had contributed so much of genius and patriotic fire to the freedom and future greatness of his country--so much to the happiness of his countrymen.

On the 24th of the month the body of Mr. Otis was taken to Boston and was placed in modest state in his former home. The funeral on the 25th was conducted by the Brotherhood of Free and Accepted Masons to which Mr. Otis belonged. The sepulture was made, as narrated in the first pages of this monograph, in the Cunningham tomb in the Old Granary Burying Ground. In that tomb, also was laid six years afterwards, the body of Ruth Cunningham Otis, his wife. Out of this brief narrative of a great life, let each reader for himself deduce as he may, the inspiration and purpose, without which American citizenship is no better that some other.

Since the first pages of this monograph were written (in March 1898,) the Sons of the American Revolution have marked the grave of James Otis with a bronze reproduction of their armorial badge, and a small tablet, as seen in the Illustration on this page.

[1] John Adams attempts to classify the pre-revolutionary orators of New England according to their ardor and influence. "The characters," says he, "the most conspicuous, the most ardent and influential, from 1760 to 1766, were first and foremost, above all and over all, James Otis; next to him was Oxenbridge Thatcher, next to him Samuel Adams; next to him, John Hancock,

then Doctor Mayhew."--Works of John Adams, Vol. X, p. 284.

If we should insert in this list the name of John Adams himself his place would be between his cousin and Hancock.

[2] In a further discussion of the prerogatives of the crown Mr. Otis said: "When the Parliament shall think fit to allow the colonists a representation in the House of Commons, the equity of their taxing the colonists will be as clear as their power is, at present, of doing it if they please."

THE CHARACTER OF JAMES OTIS BY CHARLES K. EDMUNDS, PH. D.

In viewing Washington as the "Father" of our country, as he certainly was in a sense which we of to-day are coming more and more to appreciate, in classing Hamilton and Jefferson as brothers of Washington in his great work, and in ascribing to Franklin even a greater share in establishing "The United States of America" than to any of these three, we are apt to forget those patriots who did so much to keep alive the spirit of liberty and justice in our land during the troublesome times preceding the actual rupture between England and her American Colonies. While we ascribe great and merited praise to those who not only helped to lay the foundation but also actually began to build the superstructure of our nationhood, let us not forget those who by reason of the slightly earlier day in which they strove needed even a clearer vision to follow the same plans. They labored before the day had dawned, and yet they held ever before them the same high-minded general principles of liberty and justice which actuated the lives of those who took up their work after them, when the light of Independence was fast breaking on our shores. Among these pre-revolutionists there is none more worthy of remembrance and admiration than James Otis, the foremost advocate of his time in the Colonies. Very vigorously he toiled in sowing seed the fruits of which he himself was not to see, but which under the nurture of other able hands and in the providence of the God of Nations budded at last into "The Great Republic." Thus it becomes the purpose of this article to recall briefly the most striking characteristics of him whose name must always be intimately associated with the ardent debates and the troublesome events which foreshadowed the great struggle between the greatest of colonizing nations and her greatest Colonies.

The exigency of these times was great; and men of courage and capacity, wise in council and prompt in action rose to meet it. They were not men ennobled merely by their appearance on the stage at the time when great scenes were passing. They took a part in those scenes with a degree of aptness and energy proportional to the magnitude of the occasion and throughout displayed high qualities of character.

Otis's part was played not so much in the revolution itself, as in the agitations and controversies by which it was heralded and its way prepared. "Admirably fitted by his popular talents, legal acquirements, and ardent temperament, to take an active share in the discussion respecting the comparative rights of the Colonies and the British Parliament, and in preparing the minds of his countrymen for the great step of a final separation from England, and having exhausted, as it were, his mental powers in this preparatory effort, his mind was darkened when the contest really came, and he remained an impotent spectator of the struggle, by which the liberties of his native land were at last permanently established."

The Life of James Otis as narrated by William Tudor is one of the most pleasant and instructive in the whole range of American biographies, and leaves few particulars in the personal life of Otis to be gathered by the subsequent investigator. The sketch by Francis Bowen in Jared Sparks' Library of American Biography furnishes additional and valuable illustrations of the character and services of Otis, which were secured from the third volume of Thomas Hutchinson's History of Massachusetts, (first published after Tudor's Life of Otis appeared), from the copies of papers in the office of the English Board of Trade relating to the colonial history of Massachusetts, and from the private correspondence of Governors Bernard and Hutchinson with the English Ministry, during the time of Otis's public career. These sources throw much light on the conduct of Otis as the chief political opponent of the these two colonial executives.

It is the purpose of the present article merely to emphasize the three striking traits of his character,--his impetuosity and earnestness, his high integrity and devotion to truth and justice, and his marked ability as an advocate before the bar.

In reading the memoirs of James Otis one is struck from first to last with the impetuosity, the earnestness, the ardent temper of his nature. This was at once the secret of a great measure of his power and also the partial source of his mental undoing. As a student at Harvard, the last two years of his college life were marked with great assiduity in study, and while at home during the vacations in this period, he devoted himself so closely to his books, that he was seldom seen by his friends, and often it was not known that he had returned, till he had been in his father's house for some days. Such severe application doubtless served to sow the first seeds of mental derangement, which falling on the fertile soil of his feverish disposition and nutured by the constant and intense argumentative strife of his later political career, finally found their fruition in the mental collapse which so distressingly darkened his latter days. When participating in the common amusements of youth he exhibited all the vivacity of an excitable temperament.

The earnestness of his nature led him to resign a lucrative office, renounce the favor of government, abandon the fairest prospects of professional emolument and distinction, and to devote himself to the service of his country with unflinching courage, quenchless zeal, and untiring energy.

As an orator the impetuosity of his speech and the earnestness of his voice and manner were so impressive, that they forced conviction upon his hearers even when his arguments did not reach their judgment. Such was the fluency and animation of his language, whether written or spoken, that though it was sometimes coarse and defective in taste, it was always, as will be seen from the examples quoted in this paper, extremely effective.

In political controversy the impetuosity of his nature led him to be irascible and harsh towards his opponents and sometimes hasty in judgment. But towards those whom he liked he was equally effusive in expressions of regard, and was generous, high-spirited and placable.

The fiery and impetuous temper of Otis is well illustrated by the following anecdote given by Tudor, who, however, does not vouch for its authenticity. Upon first taking his seat in the house, a friend sitting near, said: "Mr. Otis, you have great abilities, but are too warm, too impetuous; your opponents, though they cannot meet you in argument, will get the advantage by interrupting you, and putting you in a passion." "Well," said Otis, "if you see me growing warm, give me a hint, and I'll command myself." Later on when a question of some importance arose, Otis and this friend were on the Boston seat together. Otis said he was going to speak, and his companion again warned him against being irritated by interruptions from the opposition.

He soon rose, and was speaking with great fluency and powerful logic, when Timothy Ruggles interrupted him; he grew warm in reply, and his friend pulled his coat slightly. Otis scowled as he turned round, but taking the hint moderated his tone. Soon afterwards, Mr. Choate, of Ipswich, broke in on him again. This aroused his temper, and his coat was pulled a second time; turning round quickly he said in an undertone to his monitor, "Let me alone; do you take me for a schoolboy?" and continuing his address with great impetuosity he overwhelmed his opponent with sarcasm and invective.

Without doubt James Otis was a strong man,--a man of strong and positive character, whose friends and enemies were equally strong in their feelings of like and dislike. The men who were ranged as his enemies have for the most part been relegated to a second place on the page of history (this does not apply to Thomas Hutchinson, who in his official capacity was Otis's chief political opponent, but who did not exhibit the personal enemity of Bernard and others); while those who were his friends stand out boldly among the notable characters of the past. As Otis himself remarked concerning Charles Lee, we are not at a loss to know which is the highest evidence of his virtues-- the greatness and number of his friends, or the malice and envy of his foes. But friends and foes alike agree in ascribing to him a very ardent temperament, though with the latter it is unjustly regarded as violent. There is a great contrast between the estimate of Otis given by Hutchinson (quoted below) and that exhibited in the following extract from a long letter written by Governor Bernard to Lord Shelburne, near the end of the year 1766, which is entirely filled with a review of Otis's career and character, and is a curious specimen of studied calumniation. The introductory remarks show sufficiently well the spirit of the whole. "I would avoid personalities, but in the present case it is impossible. The troubles in this country take their rise from, and owe their continuance to, one man, so much, that this history alone would contain a full account of them. This man, James Otis, Esq., was a lawyer at Boston when I first came to the government. He is by nature a passionate, violent, and desperate man, which qualities sometimes work him up to an absolute frenzy.--I say nothing of him, which is not known to be his certain character, confirmed by frequent experience."

While sympathy for Otis made the public commonly ascribe the alienation of his reason chiefly to the injuries received during his encounter with Robinson in the British Coffee House, it is fairly certain that the commencement of the disease dates further back, and that the blows on the head hastened and aggravated an already incipient malady superinduced by very different causes.

In the ardor and assiduity of his devotion to the colonial cause Otis had overtaxed his mental powers. His fine faculties that had been exerted so strenuously, and with such striking effect, in the service of his country, were sinking under the excitement and the effort which had sustained them in the heat of action. For ten years he had abandoned the ordinary practice of his profession and renouncing all recreation had given his entire time and thought, himself, verily, to the "great argument" which involved the welfare of the Colonies, and as we now see it, of the world. To allow one idea exclusive occupancy of the mind and constantly to ponder a single topic, is a very frequent and almost sure cause of mental distress. It was his highest merit and at the same time his greatest misfortune, that Otis permitted this political controversy to have such an absorbing and despotic command of his attention that melancholy consequences gradually appeared and left little hope of his final restoration. His excitable and passionate temperament allowed the fire to be soon kindled, and nourished the flame in which his intellect, strong as it had been, was ultimately destroyed.

Otis's mental malady first appeared in a form which was mistaken for mere eccentricity of humor, and some time elapsed before his oddities of fancy and conduct deepened into acknowledged insanity. An incident which might have aroused the suspicions of his friends occurred during the legislative session of 1769, when at the close of a powerful and ingenious speech by Brigadier Ruggles in which he had made a deep impression, Otis at once arose and in an impassioned tone and manner which struck awe upon all those present, exclaimed, "Mr. Speaker, the liberty of this country is gone forever, and I'll go after it;" and turning round immediately left the House. Some members stared, some laughed, but none seemed to suspect the true cause of this odd behavior.

How, after the encounter with Robinson, this mental disease made inroads on his fine powers, we best know from John Adams, who on September 3,

1769, wrote: "Otis talks all; he grows the most talkative man alive; no other gentleman in company can find space to put in a word. He grows narrative like an old man." On September 5th occurred the encounter with Robinson, one of the Commissioners of Customs, at the British Coffee House, which greatly aggravated his mental disorder. From this time on he was a subject of some perplexity to the Whig leaders, though the spell with which he influenced the people was long in breaking. On January 16, Adams again wrote: "Otis is in confusion yet; he loses himself; he rambles and wanders like a ship without a helm; attempted to tell a story which took up almost all the evening. * * * In one word, Otis will spoil the club. He talks so much, and takes up so much of our time, and fills it with trash, obsceneness, profaneness, nonsense, and distraction, that we have none left for rational amusements or inquiries. * * * I fear, I tremble, I mourn, for the man and for his country; many others mourn over him with tears in their eyes."

In connection with Otis's charge against Hutchinson as to rapacious office-seeking the following extract from John Adams's diary is of curious interest. After detailing certain detractions of which he had been the victim, the diarist breaks out testily: "This is the rant of Mr. Otis concerning me. * * * But be it known to Mr. Otis I have been in the public cause as long as he, though I was never in the General Court but one year.

I have sacrificed as much to it as he. I have never got my father chosen Speaker and Counselor by it; my brother-in-law chosen into the House and chosen Speaker by it; nor a brother-in-law's brother-in-law into the House and Council by it; nor did I ever turn about in the House, and rant it on the side of the prerogative for a whole year, to get a father into a Probate office first Justice of a Court of Common Pleas, and a brother into a clerk's office. There is a complication of malice, envy, and jealousy in this man, in the present disordered state of his mind, which is quite shocking." (Oct. 27, 1772.)

In this incapacity of Otis, who at last had to seek confinement, Samuel Adams came to the front of the opposition to Hutchinson as representing the government policy, and in nothing did he show more adroitness than in the manner in which he humored and exploited the colleague, whom, though sick, the people would not suffer to be withdrawn, as is shown by the following resolution:

RESOLUTION ADOPTED AT A TOWN MEETING IN BOSTON, MAY 8, 1770.

"The Honorable James Otis having, by advice of his physician, retired into the country for the recovery of his health; Voted, That thanks of the town be given to the Honorable James Otis for the great and important services, which, as a representative in the General Assembly through a course of years, he has rendered to this town and province, particularly for his undaunted exertions in the common cause of the Colonies, from the beginning of the present glorious struggle for the rights of the British consituation. At the same time, the town cannot but express their ardent wishes for the recovery of his health, and the continuance of those public services, that must long be remembered with gratitude, and distinguish his name among the patriots of America."

During short periods of sanity, or of only partial aberration, Otis's wit and humor, rendered more quaint and striking by the peculiarities of his mental condition, made him the delight of a small circle of friends. The following anecdote, admirably told by President Adams, presents in a very graphic manner the peculiarities of his character:

"Otis belonged to a club, who met on evenings; of which club William Molineux was a member. Molineux had a petition before the legislature, which did not succeed to his wishes, and he became for several evenings sour, and wearied the company with his complaints of services, losses, sacrifices, etc., and said, 'That a man who has behaved as I have, should be treated as I am, is intolerable,' etc. Otis had said nothing; but the company were disgusted and out of patience, when Otis rose from his seat, and said, 'Come, come, Will, quit this subject, and let us enjoy ourselves; I also have a list of grievances; will you hear it?' The club expected some fun, and all cried out, 'Ay! ay! let us hear your list.'

"'Well, then, Will; in the first place, I resigned the office of the Advocate-General, which I held from the crown, that produced me--how much do you think?' 'A great deal, no doubt,' said Molineux. 'Shall we say two hundred sterling a year?' 'Ay, more I believe,' said Molineux. 'Well, let it be two hundred; that for ten years, is two thousand. In the next place, I have been obliged to relinquish the greatest part of my business at the bar. Will you set that at two hundred more?' 'O, I believe it much more than that.' 'Well, let it be two hundred; this, for ten years, is two thousand. You allow, then, I have lost four thousand pounds sterling?' 'Ay, and much more, too,' said Molineux.

"'In the next place, I have lost a hundred friends; among whom were the men of the first rank, fortune, and power, in the province. At what price will you estimate them?' 'D--n them,' said Molineux; 'at nothing: you are better without them than with them.' A loud laugh. 'Be it so,' said Otis.

"'In the next place, I have made a thousand enemies; among whom are the government of the province and the nation. What do you think of this item?' 'That is as it may happen,' said Molineux.

"'In the next place, you know, I love pleasure; but I have renounced all amusement for ten years. What is that worth to a man of pleasure?' 'No great matter,' said Molineux; 'you have made politics your amusement.' A hearty laugh.

"'In the next place, I have ruined as fine health, and as good a constitution of body, as nature ever gave to man.' 'This is melancholy indeed,' said Molineux; 'there is nothing to be said on that point.'

"'Once more,' said Otis, holding his head down before Molineux; 'look upon this head!' (Where was a scar in which a man might bury his finger.) 'What do you think of this? And, what is worse, my friends think I have a monstrous crack in my skull.'

"This made all the company very grave, and look very solemn. But Otis, setting up a laugh, and with a gay countenance, said to Molineux, 'Now, Willy, my advice to you is, to say no more about your grievances; for you and I had better put up our accounts of profit and loss in our pockets, and say no more about them, lest the world should laugh at us.'"

This whimsical dialogue put all the company, including Molineux, in a good humor, and they passed the rest of the evening very pleasantly.

One of the few fragments in Otis' handwriting now extant, is a memorandum made during the two years of transient sanity just preceding his tragic death. Returning one Sunday from public worship, he wrote: "I have this day attended divine service, and heard a sensible discourse; and thanks be to God, I now enjoy the greatest of all blessings, mens sana in copore sano" (a sound mind in a sound body). But this gleam of reason was as transient as others that had preceded, and with Bowen we willingly draw a veil over the sad record of this most terrible misfortune of our hero. "To be among men, and yet not of them; to preserve the outward form and lineaments of a human being, while the spirit within is wanting, or is transformed into a wreck of what it has been; is surely one of the most impressive and affecting instances of the ills to which mortality is exposed. It enforces with melancholy earnestness the moral lesson, that the only objects of the affections are the character and the intellect; and when these are destroyed, we look upon the external shape and features only as on the tomb in which the mortal remains of a friend repose. We even long for the closing of the scene, and think it would be far better if the now tenantless and ruined house were levelled with the ground."

A nice sense of honor was perhaps the second most striking point in Otis's energetic and strongly-marked character. Called by reason of his fame as an advocate to the management of suits even at a distance from home, and receiving the largest fees ever given to an advocate in the province, he yet disdained to suffer the success of any of his cases to rest on any petty arts or undue evasions. Conscious of possessing eminent abilities and sufficient learning he undertook to advocate no cause that he did not truly and fully believe in. His ardent pleading and the fairness of his dealing before the courts was the result of his firm belief in the justice of his cause. Nothing but truth could give him this firmness; but plain truth and clear evidence can be beat down by no ability in handling the quirks and substitutes of the law.

It was from this source as from no other that Otis drew his power as a pleader. He was as John Adams records concerning his speech on the "Writs of Assistance," "a flame of fire," but he was a flame of fire set burning to consume the dross of injustice and to purify and rescue the gold of liberty and fair-dealing. Thomas Hutchinson, before whom Otis often pleaded and whose testimony is of the greatest weight when we remember that Otis was his political opponent, has said that he never knew fairer or more noble conduct in a pleader than in Otis; that he always disdained to take advantage of any clerical error or similar inadvertence, but passed over minor points, and defended his causes solely on their broad and substantial foundations. In this regard Otis seems to satisfy Emerson's definition of a great man, when in his essay on the "Uses of Great Men" the latter declares: "I count him a great man who inhabits a higher sphere of thought, into which other men rise with labor and difficulty; he has but to open his eyes to see things in a true light, and in large relations; whilst they must make painful corrections, and keep a vigilant eye on many sources of error."

Indeed, it can be said of Otis as Coleridge said of O'Connell, "See how triumphant in debate and action he is. And why? Because he asserts a broad principle, acts up to it, rests his body upon it, and has faith in it." The world is upheld, as Emerson says, by the veracity of good men; and so the great power of Otis as an advocate before the civil bar in the minor cases of his career, and as an advocate of the people in the larger court in the great case of his life, for the liberty of opposing arbitrary power by speaking and writing the truth, arose almost entirely from his absolute integrity and fairmindedness. Clarendon's portrait of Falkland applies equally as well to Otis, --"He was so severe an adorer of the truth that he could as easily have given himself leave to steal as to dissemble." In short, Otis acted aright, and feared not the consequences, and thus became a power in the community because of his personal character.

The great popularity that he immediately acquired he used for no sinister or selfish ends. He stooped to none of the arts of the demagogue; he was never carried away by a blind spirit of faction. He opposed the arbitrary design of the English ministry with great spirit and firmness, though with some indiscretion; but he was no advocate of turbulent dissensions or causeless revolt. He allowed himself to be ruled by the greater moderation and prudence of his associates, while he inspired them with his own resistless energy and determination.

No imputation can justly be thrown on the sincerity of his patriotism, although the attempt was made by some of his contemporaries.

When in 1764, Otis, as chairman of a committee of the Assembly appointed to consider the status of the Sugar Act, favored the commission of Hutchinson as a special agent of the Colony to go to England and present the claims of the colonists, he was accused of inconsistency in opinion and action, and of dereliction of duty as the acknowledged leader of the patriotic party.

Combined with the extraordinary appointment of Hutchinson, which however never took effect owing to the opposition of Governor Bernard, Otis was also charged with a too absolute recognition of the supremacy of Parliament in his pamphlet on the Rights of the Colonies. As his father had recently received a judicial appointment, of no great importance, however, some persons went so far as to suspect Otis's fidelity to the cause, among whom was John Adams, as we see from his diary quoted elsewhere in this paper. People talked of a compromise in which he was supposed to be engaged for gradually withdrawing all resistance to the proceedings of the ministry.

Such charges, however, were but the indications of the unsteadiness and injustice of fickle popular favor. The sacrifices which Otis made for the cause, as told of by himself in the narrative given in this paper, were far too heavy for his patriotism to be doubted for an instant, and any remaining doubt must certainly be removed by a glance at the official correspondence of Governor Bernard in which he is from first to last regarded as the chief opponent of the prerogative and is subjected to much calumny on that account.

The selection of Lieutenant-Governor Hutchinson as the special agent of the Colony, though appearing at first sight somewhat strange, is easily explained and appears as the best possible choice. He was a native of the province, and as such thoroughly acquainted with its interests and desirous of promoting them. A few years before he had given sound advice to both Houses in relation to the very matter of the Sugar Act, counselling them not to apply for a reduction of the duty, lest they should appear as indirectly consenting to pay it under any circumstances; advice which had prevailed against the preconceived opinion of a majority of both branches of the legislature. Moreover, Hutchinson's attachment to the interests of the crown, and his intimate relations with the ministry, would enable him to prosecute the suit of the province to great advantage, whereas a known leader of the popular party in Massachusetts would not be received with much favor at the Board of Trade, whatever his errand.

As to Otis's rather unstinted recognition of the prerogatives of the crown and the right of Parliament to tax the Colonies, we remark that he had undoubtedly the same ends in view as the other popular leaders, but he differed from them in the choice of the means, the selection of arguments, and the proper mode of conducting the controversy. All certainly desired to be exempt from taxation and to secure freedom of trade; the question was how best attain these ends and reconcile their pretensions with the acknowledged principles of English law? Otis opposed both the Sugar Act and the Stamp Act on the same broad principle on which Hampden in England resisted the payment of ship-money, namely, that neither measure was sanctioned by the representatives of the people on whom these contributions for the support of the government were to be levied. He was too good a lawyer to question openly the abstract supremacy of Parliament, or to deny the technical "right" of this body to tax America, or to do anything else. But he affirmed that he could not justifiably exercise this right unless representatives elected by America were admitted to sit in the House of Commons. "When Parliament," said he, "shall think fit to allow the colonists a representation in the House of Commons, the equity of their taxing the colonists will be as clear as their power is at present of doing it, if they please." These opinions did not coincide with the sentiments of the greater part of the people at this period, and they were displeased with the explicit and comprehensive terms in which Otis acknowledged the authority of Parliament; they did not care to be reminded of their subjection in such positive language. Otis's incautious use of words may have led him to exaggerate the sovereignty of England over her Colonies, but the course which he pursued was undoubtedly the most judicious one for the interests of America.

That this criticism and disaffection concerning Otis was of short duration, and justly so, is shown by the fact that at the end of the legislative session he was appointed chairman of the committee charged with securing the co-operation of the other Colonies in a united effort of opposition to the scheme for taxing America. That he was sufficiently alive to the true interests of the Colonies and watchful of any imposition upon their rights as subjects under the English Constitution, we may cite one or two brief extracts from the letter of instructions to the provincial agent in England, written by him and adopted by the representatives. "The silence of the province," he says in regard to the Sugar Act, "should have been imputed to any cause, even to despair, rather than be construed into tacit cession of their rights, or an acknowledgment of a right in the Parliament of Great Britain to impose duties and taxes upon a people, who are not represented in the House of Commons." "Ireland is a conquered country, which is not the case with the northern Colonies, except Canada; yet no duties have been levied by the British Parliament on Ireland.

No internal or external taxes have been assessed on them, but by their own Parliament."

"Granting that the time may come, which we hope is far off, when the British Parliament shall think fit to oblige the North Americans, not only to maintain civil government among themselves, for this they have already done, but to support an army to protect them, can it be possible that the duties to be imposed and the taxes to be levied shall be assessed without the voice or consent of one American in Parliament? If we are not represented, we are slaves."

The charge that Otis turned from his support of the government policy because his father failed to receive the desired appointment as Chief Justice is as unfounded as it is improbable.

The office of Chief Justice was worth not over a hundred and twenty pounds sterling a year, and as Colonel Otis's practice at the bar was worth much more than this, and his seat in the legislature gave him all the power and reputation he needed, the loss of the Chief Justiceship could not have been a very great concern to him. On the other hand one of the first measures of Otis in coming into public life was to resign his office as Advocate-General which was worth twice as much as the seat on the bench. Of course a person of his fiery disposition felt keenly the insult involved in the rejection of his father, and doubtless the event imbittered his language towards Hutchinson; but it would hardly be likely to shape his whole political career when public questions of such great moment were at stake.

There was no trace of meanness or selfishness in his disposition.

To be sure, Otis's admitted superiority over his legal associates and the natural impetuosity of his nature sometimes made him excessively dogmatic, and his manner though courteous even to a fineness towards those whom he liked was imperious and even unguarded toward his political enemies. At one time, having cited Dormat (the noted French jurist, 1625-1696, author of "The Civil Laws in their Natural Order," 1689) in the course of an argument, Governor Bernard inquired "who Dormat was." Otis answered that "he was a very distinguished civilian, and not the less an authority for being unknown to your excellency." Yet notice the high-minded courtesy exhibited in the following incident: When Charles Lee was in command of the left wing of the army with his headquarters at Winter Hill, in what is now Somerville, he refused to have an interview and conference with his old friend Burgoyne, then lately arrived in Boston, looking toward the restoration of an amicable understanding between the colonies and the mother country. Four months later, a letter came from the Old World containing a warning that Lee was not a man of trustworthy character. Otis was at that time the executive head of the provisional government which had been formed in Massachusetts, during one of the last of his lucid intervals. On behalf of the government he sent a letter to Lee, quite touching for its fairminded simplicity. The council had come into possesssion of a letter from Ireland making very unfavorable mention of Lee. It produced no impression upon the council. "On the contrary," says Otis, "we are at a loss to know which is the highest evidence of your virtues--the greatness and number of your friends, or the malice and envy of your foes." This was a most delicate and effective way of offering good advice.

When he had suffered so cruelly at the hands of Commissioner Robinson and his companions at the British Coffee House, and had been awarded damages by the court, Otis's high spirit revolted at the idea of receiving pecuniary compensation for a personal insult; and Robinson's release drawn up by Otis himself is to be found in the files of the Supreme Judicial Court of Massachusetts, along with Robinson's written acknowledgment and apology.

Next to his impetuous devotion to the true relations of things, the source of Otis's power lay in his adequate preparation for the life of an advocate. Bred to the law at a time long before the pathway had been smoothed by the multiplication of elementary works and other modern improvements, he yet fully mastered that abstruse science, which perhaps does more to quicken and invigorate the understanding than many of the other kinds of learning put together. As a sufficient foundation for his later legal studies he had pursued at Harvard, the foremost college in the colonies, not only the regular undergraduate classical course, but also the three years of work required for the Master's degree. Moreover, in conformity with his views on the necessity of a generous and comprehensive culture of the mind as a means of success at the bar, or in any professional career, Otis did not plunge at once from his collegiate courses into the routine of the legal office; but allowed himself two years of self-directed general study with a view toward further disciplining his mind and widening his information. The subjects thus pursued and the general culture which he acquired served to open and to liberalize his mind in nearly the same proportion as the assiduous study of the law was next to invigorate and quicken it. In conversation with his brother he remarked, "that Blackstone's Commentaries would have saved him seven years' labor pouring over and delving in black letter." He appears to have formed a very correct judgment respecting the nature of professional education and the best means of mastering its abstruse details. He constantly inculcated upon the young men who came to study in his office the maxim, "that a lawyer ought never to be without a volume of natural or public law, or moral philosophy, on his table or in his pocket."

After two years of practice in Plymouth, he removed to Boston (1750), where he found the larger field which was demanded by his superior training and abilities; and he very soon rose to the front rank of his profession.

The regard which he entertained for his master in the law is well shown by his conduct as the opposing advocate during the hearing on the Writs of Assistance, when Otis having resigned his post of Advocate-General of the Province in order to champion the people's cause, the vacancy was filled by the appointment of Gridley. Otis held the character and abilities of his former teacher in very high respect, and allowed this differential feeling to appear throughout the trial. "It was," says John Adams, who was present on this occasion, and from whom nearly all the details of the course of this affair are derived, "it was a moral spectacle more affecting to me than any I have ever seen upon the stage, to observe a pupil treating his master with all the deference, respect, esteem, and affection of a son to a father, and that without the least affectation; while he baffled and confounded all his authorities, confuted all his arguments, and reduced him to silence." Nor was a suitable return wanting on the part of Mr. Gridley, who "seemed to me to exult inwardly at the glory and triumph of his pupil."

Though he made no pretensions to scholarship, some of his writings showed a cultivated taste and a love of literary pursuits, which were gratified so far as his numerous engagements in public service would permit. With a literary taste formed and matured by the study of Latin and Greek prosidy as constituted in the best models of antiquity, it is not surprising that his opinions on matters of criticism and scholarship were those of the Odd school, and that he decried all the forms of innovation in letters which had begun to show themselves in his day, and which he regarded as affectations. His constant advice to young people was if you want to read poetry, read Shakespeare, Milton, Dryden, and Pope; throw all the rest in the fire. And with the addition of but one or two names which have appeared since his time, such counsel is judicious advice even to-day.

His abilities were, perhaps, somewhat overrated in the admiring judgment of his contemporaries. His style as a writer was copious and energetic; but it was sometimes careless, coarse and even incorrect. His eloquence was better adapted to popular assemblies than to the graver occasions of legislative debate; in the halls of justice, it produced a greater effect on the jury than on the judge. "The few fragments of his speeches that were reported and are now extant give no idea of the enthusiasm that was created by their delivery. The elevation of his mind, and the known integrity of his purposes, enabled him to speak with decision and dignity, and commanded the respect as well as the admiration of his audience." While his arguments were sometimes comprehensive and varied, they generally related only to a few points which they placed in a very clear and convincing light. His object was immediate effect. He had studied the art of clear expression and forcible argument in order to act with facility and force upon the minds of others to such an extent as to convince them, and then to convert their conviction into action. He employed the facility and the power thus gained not for any personal agrandizement, but to advocate political reform for the good of the whole people.

In the latter part of his speech on the Writs of Assistance, he discussed the incompatibility of the acts of trade as lately adopted by the English Ministry with the charter of the colony. In so doing "he reproached the nation, Parliament, and King," says John Adams, "with injustice, illiberality, ingratitude, and oppression, in their conduct towards the people of this country, in a style of oratory that I never heard equalled in this or any other country." As to the effect of this oration in increasing the courage of the colonists, inciting them to scrutinize more closely and resist more strenuously, the claims of the British Ministry and Parliament, we have Adams's significant statement,-- "I do say in the most solemn manner that Mr. Otis's oration against Writs of Assistance breathed into this nation the breath of life."

The longest and most elaborate production from his pen is the pamphlet on the "Rights of the Colonies." It affords a fair specimen of his impetuous and inaccurate rhetoric, his rapid and eager manner of accumulating facts, arguments, and daring assertions, and the "glowing earnestness and depth of patriotic feeling with which all his compositions are animated." It is not surprising that a book written in this style caused the author to be suspected of wildness and even of madness. But there was, as Bowen remarks, a method and a good deal of logical power in his madness.

The pamphlet was reprinted, circulated, and read in Great Britain and even attracted the attention of the House of Lords. In February, 1766, during a debate in that body on the disturbances in America, Lord Littleton made some allusion to the peculiar opinions of Mr. Otis, and spoke slightingly of his book. Lord Mansfield replied, "With respect to what has been said, or written, upon this subject, I differ from the noble Lord, who spoke of Mr. Otis and his book with contempt, though he maintained the same doctrine in some points, although, in others, he carried it further than Otis himself, who allows everywhere the supremacy of the crown over the colonies. No man on such a subject is contemptible. Otis is a man of consequence among the people there. They have chosen him for one of their deputies at the Congress, and general meeting from the respective governments. It was said the man is mad. What then? One madman often makes many. Massaniello was mad, no body doubts; yet for all that, he overturned the government of Naples. Madness is catching in all popular assemblies, and upon all popular matters.

The book is full of wildness. I never read it till a few days ago, for I seldom look into such things."

In some of his arguments he lays down general principles with a quaint extravagance which marks the peculiar humor of the man. "No government has the right to make hobby-horses, asses, and slaves of the subject; nature having made sufficient of the two former, for all the lawful purposes of man, from the harmless peasant in the field to the most refined politician in the cabinet; but none of the last, which infallibly proves that they are unnecessary." "The British constitution of government as now established in his Majesty's person and family, is the wisest and best in the world. The King of Great Britain is the best as well as the most glorious monarch upon the globe, and his subjects the happiest in the universe. The French King is a despotic, arbitrary prince, and, consequently, his subjects are very miserable." The last specimen which we shall quote comes from his defence of the objectionable passage in the remonstrance drawn up by Otis on behalf of the Assembly of 1762 against Governor Bernard's conduct in increasing the expenses of the colony without previously obtaining the consent of the Legislature. This passage was as follows: "No necessity can be sufficient to justify a House of Representatives in giving up such a privilege; for it would be of little consequence to the people, whether they were subject to George or Louis, the King of Great Britain or the French King, if both were arbitrary, as both would be, if both could levy taxes without Parliament." Afterwards in commenting on this passage he made the following defense of its apparent unpatriotic sentiment. "It may be objected, that there are some differences between arbitrary princes, in this respect, at least, that some are more rigorous than others. It is granted; but, then, let it be remembered, that the life of man is a vapor that soon vanisheth away, and we know not who may come after him, a wise man or a fool; though the chances, before and since Solomon, have ever been in favor of the latter."--"That I should die very soon after my head should be struck off, whether by a sabre or a broadsword, whether chopped off to gratify a tyrant by the Christian name of Tom, Dick, or Harry, is evident. That the name of the tyrant would be of no more avail to save my life, than the name of the executioner, needs no proof. It is, therefore, manifestly of no importance what a prince's Christian name is, if he be arbitrary, any more, indeed, than if he were not arbitrary. So the whole amount of this dangerous proposition may, at least in one view, be reduced to this, viz.: It is of little importance what a king's Christian name is. It is, indeed, of importance, that a king, a governor, and all good Christians, should have a Christian name; but whether Edward, Francis, or William, is of none, that I can discern."

A passage ascribed to Otis during a session of the legislature at Cambridge gives some idea of the character of his invective. It had been said in defence of some measure that it had been taken by the advice of Council, when Otis exclaimed, "Ay, by the advice of Council, forsooth! And so it goes, and so we are to be ruined! The Council are governed by his Excellency, his Excellency by Lord Hillsborough, Lord Hillsborough by his Majesty, his Majesty by Lord Bute, and Lord Bute by the Lord knows who. This recalls to mind what used to be said when I was a student in this place. It was observed at that time, that the President directed the scholars how they should act, madame directed the President, Titus, their black servant, governed madame, and the devil prompted Titus."

The most comprehensive and just appreciation of the character and work of Otis is given us by Francis Bowen in Jared Spark's Library of American Biography. In part he says: "The services which Mr. Otis rendered to this country were so conspicuous and important, that it is difficult to form an estimate of his character with the impartiality that history requires. Gratitude might justly efface the memory of his faults from the minds of those who have profited so largely by his patriotism and his virtues. But it is not necessary thus to seek excuses for his failings, or reasons for covering up the errors that he committed. The defects of his temperament and conduct may be freely mentioned, for they are not such as materially lessen our respect for him as a man. * * * * * * * * * * * "As the vindicator of American rights, during the period of colonial subordination, as the acknowledged leader, in Massachusetts, of the constitutional opposition to ministerial influence and parliamentary usurpation, the services of Mr. Otis cannot be too highly appreciated. * * * * * * * * * * * "He was not permitted to witness the grand result of his labors. He did not live to enjoy the final triumph; he can hardly be said to have survived till the opening of the struggle. But the historian who searches into the causes of this great event, and seeks to determine the comparative merits of the men who achieved it, will dwell long upon the services, and pay a just tribute of admiration and respect to the memory of James Otis."

THE USE AND ABUSE OF ARBITRARY POWER, Including Tracts from Burke, Otis and Wilkes. By Charles K. Edmunds, Ph.D.

It is the honor of England that she had deposited in the virgin soil of her colonies the germ of freedom. Nearly all at their foundation, or shortly after, received charters which conferred the franchises of the mother country on the colonists. These charters were neither a vain show nor a dead letter, but really did establish and allow powerful institutions which impelled the colonists to defend their liberty, and to control the power by participating in it as constituted in the grant of supplies, the election of public councils, trial by jury, and the right of assembling to discuss the general affairs. To us of to-day these appear as common-sense or logically necessary rights; but we must remember that in those early days of colonization they were distinct privileges accorded in power to the colonists. And it is in these very privileges that we behold the germinating principle which was ultimately to bring to life the new republic then as yet unborn. For as Thomas Jefferson afterward wrote, "where every man is a sharer in the direction of his town-republic, and feels that he is a participator in the government of affairs, not merely at an election one day in the year, but every day; when there shall not be a man in the State who will not be a member of some one of its councils, great or small, he will let the heart be torn out of his body sooner than allow his power to be wrested from him by a Caesar or a Bonaparte. How powerfully did we feel the energy of this organization in the case of the embargo!"

Notwithstanding the widely different origin of the various colonists, the circumstances in which they were placed were so similar, that the same general form of personal character must inevitably have developed itself, and produced a growing consciousness of power and impatience of foreign imposition. The proximate independence of America need not have been a certainty, however, had the eyes of English statesmen not been blinded to the truth of the principles urged by such men as Otis in America and Burke in England. The causes which were to produce a final rupture were, to be sure, already at work (their full operation being delayed by the lack of union among the different provinces), but there was at the same time a warm hereditary attachment to the parent country, under whose wings the provinces had grown up, by whose arms they had been shielded, and by whose commerce, in spite of jealous restrictions, they had been enriched.

Indeed life in the Colonies was so closely related to that in the mother country that in a very marked degree, the history of the Colonies is only the more practical and laborious development of the spirit of liberty flourishing amid the conditions of life in the new country under the standard of the laws and traditions of the old country. As the eminent philosophical historian, M. Guizat, has said, "It might be considered the history of England herself." The resemblance is the more striking when we remember that the majority of the American Colonies and the more important of them were founded or increased the most rapidly at the very epoch when England was preparing to sustain, and in part already sustaining, those fierce conflicts against the pretensions of absolute power which were to obtain for her the honor of giving to the world the first example of a great nation free and well governed.

How similarly the state of affairs appeared, in the eyes of those who were not blinded by self-interest, on both sides of the Atlantic, is shown by the following extracts from Burke and Otis.

In 1770 Burke thus described the social and political conditions both at home and in the Colonies: "That the government is at once dreaded and contemned; that the laws are despoiled of all their respected and salutary terrors; that their inaction is a subject of ridicule and their enforcement of abhorrence; that rank, and office, and title, and all the solemn plausibilities of the world, have lost their reverence and effect; that our foreign politics are as much deranged as our domestic economy; that our dependencies are slackened in their affection and loosened from their obedience; that we know neither how to yield nor how to enforce; that hardly anything above or below, abroad or at home, is sound and entire; but that disconnection and confusion, in office, in parties, in families, in parliament, in the nation, prevail beyond the disorders of any former time, these are facts universally admitted and lamented."

When in 1768 troops were sent to Boston to prevent a repetition of the disturbances which had resulted from the arbitrary and insulting manner in which the commissioners of customs exercised their office, Otis was chosen moderator of the town meeting held in protest, and is reported to have declared "That in case Great Britain was not disposed to redress their grievances after proper applications, the inhabitants had nothing more to do, but to gird the sword to the thigh, and shoulder the musket." Another account presents a somewhat more temperate tone, representing Otis as "strongly recommending peace and good order, and the grievances the people labored under might in time be removed; if not, and we were called on to defend our liberties and privileges, he hoped and believed we should, one and all, resist even unto blood; but at the same time, he prayed Almighty God it might never so happen."

The change from favorable conditions both in England and in the Colonies to the state of unrest depicted by these passages from Burke and Otis, had been brought about by the attempt to use strong measures, enforced with no just regard for the welfare of the whole people. The English Ministry failed to realize that it is of the utmost importance not to make mistakes in the use of strong measures; that firmness is a virtue only when it accompanies the most perfect wisdom. Their course of political conduct, combined with the establishment of a system of favoritism both at home and abroad like that adopted by Henry the Third of France, produced results of the same kind as the latter.

Members of parliament for the most part were practically convinced that they did not depend on the affection or opinion of the people for their political being, and gave themselves over, with scarcely the appearance of reserve, to the influence of the court. There was thus developed both a ministry and parliament unconnected with the people, and we have the deplorable picture of the executive and legislative parts of a government attempting to exist apart from their true foundation--the opinion of the people. How signally such attempts have always failed is a matter of historical record. And the steadfast belief that they always will so fail constitutes the great force of public opinion to-day.

Had the English Ministry and the Colonial Governors, in particular Governor Bernard of Massachusetts, recognized certain cardinal principles of individual and national liberty, which were so strongly advocated by Burke and Otis, the course of events in their dealing with the colonists would in all probability have been greatly different from that actually developed. Burke declared that as long as reputation, the most precious possession of every individual, and as long as opinion, the great support of the state, depend entirely upon the voice of the people, the latter can never be considered as a thing of little consequence either to individuals or to governments. He pointed out that nations are governed by the same methods, and on the same principles, by which an individual without authority is often able to govern those who are his equals or even his superiors, namely, by a knowledge of their temper, and by a judicious management of it; that is, when public affairs are steadily and quietly conducted, not when government descends to a continued scuffle between the magistrate and the multitude, in which sometimes the one and sometimes the other is uppermost; each alternately yielding and prevailing in a series of contemptible victories and scandalous submissions. "The temper of the people amongst whom he presides ought, therefore, to be the first study of a statesman. And the knowledge of this temper it is by no means impossible for him to attain, if he has not an interest in being ignorant of what it is his duty to learn."

Of course it will not do to think that the people are never in the wrong. They have frequently been so, both in other countries and in England; but in all disputes between them and their rulers, the presumption is at least upon a par in favor of the people. History justifies us in going even further, for when popular discontents have been very prevalent something has generally been found amiss in the constitution, or in the conduct of the government. As Burke declares, "the people have no interest in disorder. When they do wrong, it is their error, and not their crime. But with the governing part of the state it is far otherwise. They certainly may act ill by design, as well as by mistake. * * * If this presumption in favor of the subjects against the trustees of power be not the more probable, I am sure it is the more comfortable speculation; because it is more easy to change an administration than to reform a people."

Very much the same ideas are presented by Otis in his article on the "Rights of the Colonists," and the passage bearing on this present topic will be given for comparison with Burke's treatment. The pamphlet is divided into four parts, treating respectively of the origin of government, of colonies in general, of the natural rights of colonists, and of the political and civil rights of the British colonists. The writer maintains, that government is founded not as some had supposed on compact, but as Paley afterwards affirmed, on the will of God. By the divine will, the supreme power is placed "originally and ultimately in the people; and they never did, in fact, freely, nor can they rightfully, make an absolute, unlimited renunciation of this divine right. It is ever in the nature of a thing given in trust; and on a condition the performance of which no mortal can dispense with, namely, that the person or persons, on whom the sovereignty is conferred by the people, shall incessantly consult their good. Tyranny of all kinds is to be abhorred, whether it be in the hands of one, or of the few, or of the many.

The colonies were not at all unwilling to pay revenue to the home government, if the manner of payment was just and right. They were so far from refusing to grant money that the Assembly of Pennsylvania resolved to the following effect: "That they always had, so they always should think it their duty to grant aid to the crown, according to their abilities, whenever required of them in the usual constitutional manner." This resolution was presented by Franklin, who was a member of the Pennsylvania Assembly, to the Prime Minister of England, Mr. Grenville, before the latter introduced the

Stamp Act into Parliament. Other colonies made similar resolutions, and had Grenville instead of the Stamp Act, applied to the King for proper requisitional letters to be circulated among the colonies by the Secretary of State, it is highly probable that he would have obtained more money from the colonies by their voluntary grants than he himself expected from the stamps. Such at any rate is the claim of Franklin, who was surely in a position to feel the pulse of the colonies better than any other one man. "But he (Grenville) chose compulsion rather than persuasion, and would not receive from their good-will what he thought he could obtain without it. Thus the golden bridge which the Americans were charged with unwisely and unbecomingly refusing to hold out to the minister and parliament, was actually held out to them, but they refused to walk over it."

The action of the English Ministry in the matter of the tea tax in particular, and of the whole question of American taxation in general, is thus spoken of by Burke in his famous address in the House of Commons:

"There is nothing simple, nothing manly, nothing ingenious, open, decisive, or steady, in the proceeding, with regard either to the continuance or the repeal of the taxes. The whole has an air of littleness and fraud. * * * There is no fair dealing in any part of the transaction." * * * * * * * * * * * * "No man ever doubted that the commodity of tea could bear an imposition of three-pence. But no commodity will bear three-pence, or will bear a penny, when the general feelings of men are irritated, and two millions of people are resolved not to pay. The feelings of the colonists were formerly the feelings of Great Britain. Theirs were formerly the feelings of Mr. Hampden when called upon for the payment of twenty shillings. Would twenty shillings have ruined Mr. Hampden's fortune? No, but the payment of half twenty shillings, on the principle it was demanded, would have made him a slave. * * * It is then upon the principle of this measure, and nothing else, that we are at issue." * * * * * * * * * * * "I select the obnoxious colony of Massachusetts Bay, which at this time (but without hearing her) is so heavily a culprit before parliament--I will select their proceedings even under circumstances of no small irritation. For, a little imprudently, I must say, Governor Bernard mixed in the administration of the lenitive of the repeal no small acrimony arising from matters of a separate nature. Yet see, Sir, the effect of that lenitive, though mixed with these bitter ingredients; and how this rugged people can express themselves on a measure of concession.

"'If it is not in our power,' (say they in their address to Governor Bernard), "in so full a manner as will be expected, to show our respectful gratitude to the mother country, or to make a dutiful and affectionate return to the indulgence of the king and parliament, it shall be no fault of ours; for this we intend, and hope we shall be able fully to effect.'

"Would to God that this tender had been cultivated, managed, and set in action; other effects than those which we have since felt would have resulted from it. On the requisition for compensation to those who had suffered from the violence of the populace, in the same address they say, 'The recommendation enjoined by Mr. Secretary Conway's letter, and in consequence thereof made to us, we will embrace the first convenient opportunity to consider and act upon.' They did consider; they did act upon, it. They obeyed the requisition. I know the mode has been chicaned upon, but it was substantially obeyed, and much better obeyed than I fear the parliamentary requisition of this session will be, though enforced by all your rigour, and backed with all your power. In a word, the damages of popular fury were compensated by legislative gravity. Almost every other part of America in various ways demonstrated their gratitude. I am bold to say, that so sudden a calm recovered after so violent a storm is without parallel in history. To say that no other disturbance should happen from any other cause, is folly. But as far as appearances went, by the judicious sacrifice of one law, you procured an acquiescence in all that remained. After this experience, nobody shall persuade me, when a whole people are concerned, that acts of lenity are not means of conciliation."

"OPPOSITION TO ARBITRARY POWER," By John Wilkes, 1763.

While Otis and other patriots were opposing the arbitrary measures of the English Ministry in their dealings with the Colonies, certain men in England were equally as ardent in their opposition to such a course whether pursued at home or abroad. Most prominent among these were Edmund Burke and John Wilkes, both members of Parliament. In this connection the following extracts frown Wilkes' article on "Opposition to Arbitrary Power" will be of interest. This article appeared in the famous No. 45 of "The North Briton," edited by Wilkes, who was very clever but somewhat profligate.

* * * "In vain will such a minister (referring to Lord Bute), or the foul dregs of his power, the tools of corruption and despotism, preach up in the speech that spirit of concord, and that obedience to the laws, which is essential to good order. They have sent the spirit of discord through the land, and I will prophesy, that it will never be extinguished, but by the extinction of their power. Is the spirit of concord to go hand in hand with the Peace and Excise, through this nation? Is it to be expected between an insolent Excisemen, and a peer, gentleman, freeholder, or farmer, whose private houses are now made liable to be entered and searched at pleasure? The spirit of concord hath not gone forth among men, but the spirit of liberty has, and a noble opposition has been given to the wicked instruments of oppression. A nation as sensible as the English, will see that a spirit of concord when they are oppressed, means a tame submission to injury, and that a spirit of liberty ought then to arise, and I am sure ever will, in proportion to the weight of the grievance they feel. Every legal attempt of a contrary tendency to the spirit of concord will be deemed a justifiable resistance, warranted by the spirit of the English constitution.

"A despotic minister will always endeavor to dazzle his prince with high-flown ideas of the prerogative and honor of the crown, which the minister will make a parade of firmly maintaining. I wish as much as any man in the kingdom to see the honor of the crown maintained in a manner truly becoming Royalty.

* * * * The prerogative of the crown is to exert the constitutional powers entrusted to it in a way not of blind favor and partiality, but of wisdom and judgment. This is the spirit of our constitution. The people too have their prerogative, and I hope the fine words of Dryden will be engraven on our hearts: 'Freedom is the English Subject's Prerogative.'"

JOSEPH WARREN'S OPINION OF GOVERNOR BERNARD, OTIS'S PRINCIPAL ENEMY.

Governor Bernard's bad temper and bad taste in dealing with the legislature may justly be ranked among the principal causes which gradually, but effectually, alienated the affections of the people of Massachusetts, first from the persons immediately charged with the government of the province, and finally, from the royal authority and whole English dominion. "With an arrogant and self-sufficient manner, constantly identifying himself with the authority of which he was merely the representative, and constantly indulging in irritating personal allusions, he entirely lost sight of the courtesy and respect due to a co-ordinate branch of the government, and made himself ridiculous, while he was ruining the interests of the sovereign whom he was most anxious to serve. Even Hutchinson, as we learn from the third volume of his History, though he was attached to the same policy, and favored the same measures, censures the tone of Bernard's messages as ungracious, impolitic, and offensive."

Popular animosity against Governor Bernard waxed exceedingly strong during the controversy concerning the circular letter sent by the Massachusetts Assembly to each House of Representatives in the thirteen Colonies, in which the Colonies were urged to concert a uniform plan for remonstrance against the government policy. Bernard sent advices to England declaring that stringent measures were imperative. Among those who were particularly vehement in their denunciation of Bernard's character and conduct was Joseph Warren, a young physician of twenty-seven years, Otis's brother-in-law, for some time a writer for the papers, who was even more drastic than Otis in his arraignment of Bernard's tactics as governor, and who caused somewhat of a sensation by publishing the following in the "Boston Gazette" of February 29, 1768. (Warren was killed while serving as a volunteer aide at the battle of Bunker Hill.)

"We have for a long time known your enmity to this Province. We have had full proof of your cruelty to a loyal people. No age has, perhaps, furnished a more glaring instance of obstinate perseverance in the path of malice. * * * Could you have reaped any advantage from injuring this people, there would have been some excuse for the manifold abuses with which you have loaded them. But when a diabolical thirst for mischief is the alone motive of your conduct, you must not wonder if you are treated with open dislike; for it is impossible, how much soever we endeavor it, to feel any esteem for a man like you. * * * Nothing has ever been more intolerable than your insolence upon a late occasion when you had, by your jesuitical insinuations, induced a worthy minister of state to form a most unfavorable opinion of the Province in general, and some of the most respectable inhabitants in particular. You had the effrontery to produce a letter from his Lordship as a proof of your success in calumniating us. * * * We never can treat good and patriotic rulers with too great reverence. But it is certain that men totally abandoned to wickedness can never merit our regard, be their stations ever so high.

'If such men are by God appointed, The Devil may be the Lord's anointed.' A TRUE PATRIOT.

Hutchinson tried to induce the grand jury to indict Warren for libel on account of this intemperate attack. The jury, however, returned "ignoramus," and the Governor had to bear the affront, which was but one of a series directed against him during his remaining days in America.

On the other hand, direct attacks were also made against Otis, and some were marked by scurrility and coarseness of language, which could not fail to arouse a man of his temper and fine sense of honor. How he did regard them appears from the following extract from a letter to his sister, Mrs. Warren:

"Tell my dear brother Warren to give himself no concern about the scurrilous piece in Tom Fleet's paper. It has served me as much as the song did last year. The tories are all ashamed of this, as they were of that; the author is not yet certainly known, though I think I am within a week of detecting him for certain. If I should, I shall try to cure him once for all, by stringing him up, not bodily, but in such a way as shall gibbet his memory in terrorem. It lies between Bernard, Waterhouse, and Jonathan Sewall. The first, they say, has not wit enough to write anything; the second swears off; and the third must plead guilty or not guilty as soon as I see him. Till matters are settled in England, I dare not leave this town, as men's minds are in such a situation, that every nerve is requisite to keep them from running to some irregularity and imprudence; and some are yet wishing for an opportunity to hurt the country."

OTIS'S AFFECTION FOR ENGLAND IN SPITE OF HIS OPPOSITION TO THE ARBITRARY MEASURES OF HER MINISTRY. By Charles K. Edmunds, Ph. D.

Otis defended the rights of his countrymen by vindicating their enjoyment of English liberty, not by asserting the demand for American independence. He, however, sowed the seed without knowing what kind of harvest it was to produce, for his writings and speeches did more than those of any other man toward preparing the minds of others for the final separation from England.

That such was his purpose he steadfastly repudiated, and the following quotations from his pen exhibit full well his attachment to the mother country and to the principles of her constitution.

When in January, 1763, the joyful news was received at Boston that the preliminaries of peace between Great Britain and France had been signed, and that Canada was permanently annexed to the former country, the colonists justly rejoiced, and a town meeting was held of which Otis was chosen moderator. In the course of his speech, Otis declared in his usual earnest way that "the true interests of Great Britain and her plantations are mutual, and what God in his providence united, let no man dare attempt to pull asunder." Similar sentiments expressed by other leaders among the various Colonies might be quoted. We give one more from Otis's pamphlet on the "Rights of the Colonies," published in 1765. In speaking of the colonists, he says: "Their loyalty has been abundantly proved, especially in the late war. Their affection and reverence for their mother country are unquestionable. They yield the most cheerful and ready obedience to her laws, particularly to the power of that august body, the Parliament of Great Britain, the supreme legislative of the kingdom and its dominions. These, I declare, are my own sentiments of duty and loyalty." He angrily repels the charge that the Colonies were seeking for independence, insisting that the people had a "natural and almost mechanical affection for Great Britain which they conceive under no other sense, and call by no other name, than that of home. We all think ourselves happy under Great Britain. We love, esteem, and reverence our mother country, and adore our King. And could the choice of independency be offered the colonies or subjection to Great Britain on any terms above absolute slavery, I am convinced they would accept the latter."

In 1769 he wrote: "The cause of America is, in my humble opinion, the cause of the whole British empire; an empire which, from my youth, I have been taught to love and revere, as founded in the principles of natural reason and justice, and upon the whole, best calculated for general happiness of any yet risen in the world. In this view of the British empire, my Lord, I sincerely pray for its prosperity, and sincerely lament all adverse circumstances. Situated as we are, my Lord, in the wilderness of America, a thousand leagues distant from the fountains of honor and justice, in all our distresses, we pride ourselves in loyalty to the King, and affection to the mother country."

OTIS AS A PROPHET.

Otis was not much given to general speculations upon the future; but there is something very striking in the following language, taken from his pamphlet "The Rights of the Colonies," if we consider how soon after there occurred the two great crises in the world's affairs, the American and French revolutions. "I pretend neither to the spirit of prophecy, nor to any uncommon skill in predicting a crisis; much less to tell when it begins to be nascent, or is fairly midwived into the world. But I should say the world was at the eve of the highest scene of earthly power and grandeur, that has ever yet been displayed to the view of mankind. The cards are shuffling fast through all Europe. Who will win the prize is with God. This, however, I know, detur digniori. The next universal monarchy will be favorable to the human race; for it must be founded on the principles of equity, moderation, and justice."

JAMES OTIS. [1725 - 1783.] By G. Mercer Adam[3]

The character and life-work of few men belonging to the pre-Revolutionary era are better worth studying than are those of James Otis, the patriot-orator of Massachusetts, who took so prominent a part in opposing England's obnoxious Stamp Act and in arousing the American Colonies to a sense of the outrage done them by the issue of the arbitrary Writs of Assistance. Though the records of his personal life are somewhat meagre, sufficient is known of Otis's public career to interest students of his country's history and entitle him to the admiration of all, as one of the most earnest and eloquent advocates of Liberty in the Nation's youth-time, and a sturdy and noble defender of its cause at the critical era of England's injustice and oppression. No man of the period, it may be hazarded, did more yeoman service than Otis did in the cause of American Freedom, or was more sensible of the rights of the Colonists and of the injustice done them by the Motherland in her assaults on their civil and political status in the years preceding the Revolution. Not only was he one of the most fearless asserters of the great principles for which our forefathers fought and bled, but few men better than he saw more clearly the malign character of the arbitrary acts imposed upon the Colonies that brought about separation and laid the foundation of American independence. In resisting the enforcement of these Acts, Otis was actuated not only by disinterested and patriotic motives, but by a statesmanlike discernment of their unconstitutional character and the wrong they would inflict, in being inconsistent with the foundation charter of the Massachusetts Colony. Like many of the Revolutionary fathers, Otis was not at heart a rebel, or from the outset disloyal to the Crown in its administration of the affairs of the Colonies. His occupancy of the Crown post of Advocate-General and his own well-known integrity and conscientiousness forbid that idea, not to speak of his pride in the fact that his ancestors were English and for generations had held high judicial offices and militia appointments in the gift of the King and the ministry of the period. But though by tradition and training, at the outset of his career, a subject of monarchy and a true man in his official relations with England, Otis was at the same time ardent in his interests for the wellbeing of the Colonies and zealous for their rights and privileges. When these came into conflict, the stand he took was staunchly patriotic, even to the sacrifice of his office and its emoluments; while in espousing the popular cause against the King and the ministry he stood forth, as John Adams expressed it, as "a flame of fire," full of consuming zeal for his country and an ardent upholder of its rights and prerogatives. In assuming this attitude, that Otis's zeal and energy were at times unrestrained and his language occasionally unguarded and overvehement, is doubtless true; but this was certainly excusable in a man of his ardent temperament and strength of character; while the situation of affairs was such as to call not only for patriotic enthusiasm, but for righteous indignation and heated denunciation, in a cause that stirred to the depths the heart and brain of an impetuous and commanding orator. Nor do we well to forget what this consuming, patriotic passion and heated vindication of his country's rights cost Otis, in the responsibility he felt and the solicitation he manifested, especially in the middle and later stages of his strenuous career, for the cause he had so keenly at heart. Pathetic is the story of the ailment that clouded his closing years; and only exculpatory can be the judgment now passed upon the man and his work when we consider what the strain was that he had long and anxiously borne and that revealed its effects in periods of sad mental alienation and incipient madness. To speak and write strongly on taxation and its injustice, in the case of the Colonies, might well, however, disturb the mental equilibrium of even a strong man, and the more so when actively protesting, as Otis long continued to protest, against unlawful encroachments upon the liberties of the Colonies and the other arbitrary acts that then characterized the administration of the Crown. Whatever it cost Otis personally to engage in this defence, the result, as we all now know and admit, was only and wholly beneficent--in the defeat of an unrighteous autocracy, and the emancipation of a Continent from a fettering and baleful administration.

This herald of and actor in the great drama of his time was born at West Barnstable, formerly known as the Great Marshes, in Massachusetts, on the 5th of February, 1723. He was one of thirteen children, his father being Colonel James Otis (born in 1702), the son of Judge John Otis, whose immediate ancestor had emigrated from England in the preceding century and settled in New England at the town of Hingham, calling the region after the old home of the family in the Motherland. This John Otis, who was born in A.D. 1657, became a prominent man in the Settlement, was a member of the Council of the Colony, and ultimately became Chief-Justice of the Common Pleas and Probate Court. Otis's own father (Colonel James Otis) likewise became a lawyer and publicist, a colonel in the local militia, and rose to a high post in the judiciary and was a member of the Council of Massachusetts. He married Mary Alleyne and transmitted to the future patriot, the subject of this sketch, the talents and many of the characteristics of his progenitors. A brother of our hero, Samuel Alleyne Otis, rose to prominence in the politics of the State and as Secretary of the Senate administered to Washington the oath of office as President, holding the Bible on which he was sworn as honored chief of the future nation. A sister, Mercy, an ardent and loyal patriot, married the notable republican, James Warren of Plymouth, and lived herself to write a compend of the "History of the American Revolution," together with a collection of patriotic verse.

James Otis, whom we know as one of the most eloquent orators of the Revolutionary era and an ardent promoter of American independence, was educated for his career at Harvard, which institution he entered as a freshman in 1739, having previously been prepared for college by the Rev. Jonathan Russell. His university course, so far as can be gathered from any account of it that has come down to us, was not a notable one, though he had a fair scholastic career and graduated at the age of nineteen in 1743. While popular after a fashion at college, he was a bit of a recluse and a diligent student of literature, with a predilection, it is said, for music, playing well on the violin. After graduating, he wisely spent two years in general reading before entering upon the study of the law, which he did in 1745 under James Gridley, a prominent jurist of Massachusetts and sometime

Crown Attorney-General. Three years later, he was admitted to the bar, and in 1748 began to practice his profession at Plymouth, Mass. In 1750, he removed to Boston, and there became known as an advocate of note and high promise, actuated by nice professional instincts, with a fine sense of honor, and keenly appreciating, it is recorded, his responsibilities in his relations with his clients, which led him to accept only such cases as he could conscientiously defend and take retainers from.

This characteristic scruple in the lawyer gave him a high standing in his profession, and naturally led to success at the bar, besides winning for him the respect and admiration of troops of warm and attached friends.

About this time he appears to have developed uncommon gifts as an orator, and his rather irascible nature gave scope to his keen wit and powers of sarcasm. His extensive reading and ultimate study of good literary models naturally bore fruit in the practice of the forensic art and gave him prestige at the bar, as well as, later on, in taking to public life and to the advocacy of the rights of the Colonists in the controversy with the Crown.

In 1755, when he had attained his thirtieth year, Otis married Ruth Cunningham, the daughter of an influential Boston merchant. The lady, from all accounts, was undemonstrative and devoid of her husband's patriotic ardor, traits that did not tend to domestic felicity or lead, on the wife's part, to a commanding influence over her vehement and somewhat eccentric husband. The fruit of the union was one son and two daughters. The son entered the navy, but unhappily died in his eighteenth year. One of the daughters, the elder of the two, probably under the mother's influence, angered her father by espousing the English cause and marrying a Captain Brown, a British officer on duty at Boston. The marriage was a source of irritation and unhappiness to Otis, who, after his son-in-law had fought and been wounded at Bunker Hill, withdrew with his wife to England, and was there disowned and cut off by the irate patriot, whose affection was also dried up for the erring daughter. The younger daughter, on the other hand, was a devoted and patriotic woman, who shared her father's enthusiasm for the popular cause. She married Benjamin Lincoln of Boston, but early became a widow.

By this time, Otis had become not only a man eminent in his profession in

Boston, but a powerful factor in the public life of the city. The New England commonwealth was then beginning to be greatly exercised over the aggressions of the Motherland, and this was keenly watched by Otis, who took a lively and patriotic interest in Colonial affairs. Beyond his profession, which had closely engrossed him, he had heretofore taken little part in public life; his leisure, indeed, he had employed more as a student of books rather than of national affairs, as his work on the "Rudiments of Latin Prosody," published in 1760, bears witness. As the era of a conflict with England neared, he however altered in this respect, and became a zealous advocate of non-interference on the part of the Crown in the affairs of the Colonies and an ardent protester against English oppression and injustice. Soon grievances arose in the relations between the Colonies and England which gave Otis the right to denounce the Motherland and excite dissaffection among the people of the New World. These grievances arose out of the strained commercial relations between the two countries and the attempt of England to devise and enforce irritating schemes of Colonial control. Of these causes of outcry in the New World the two chief were the revival and rigid execution of the English Navigation Acts, designed to limit the freedom of the American Colonies in trading with West Indian ports in American built vessels, and the insistence, on the part of the Crown and the British government, that the Colonies should be taxed for the partial support of English garrisons in the country. In the development of trade in the New World, the Colonies reasonably felt that they should not be harassed by the mother country, and so they permitted commerce to expand as it would; and when this was enjoined by England they naturally resented interference by her and began to evade the laws which she imposed upon the young country and bid defiance to the Crown customs officers in the measures resorted to in the way of restriction and imposed penalty. This attitude of the Colonists in ignoring or defying English laws was soon now specially emphasized when the Crown resorted to more stringent measures to curb Colonial trade and impose heavy customs duties on articles entering New World ports. Flagrant acts of evasion followed, and defiant smuggling at length brought its legal consequences--in the issue by the English Court of Exchequer of search warrants, or Writs of Assistance, as they were called, by which it was sought to put a stop to smuggling, by resorting to humiliating arbitrary measures sure to be resented by the Colonies. These Writs of Assistance empowered the King's officers, or others delegated by them, to board vessels in port and enter and search warehouses, and even the private homes of the Colonists, for contraband goods and all importations that had not paid toll to His Majesty's customs. This attempted rigid execution of the Acts of Trade, together with other arbitrary measures on the part of the Crown which followed, such as the imposition of the Stamp Act, and the coercive levy of taxes to pay part of the cost of maintaining English troops in the Colonies, was soon to cost England dear and end in the loss of her possessions in America and the rise of the New World Republic.

One of the most active men in the Colonies to oppose this Colonial policy of England was, as we know, the patriot James Otis, at the time Advocate-General of the Crown, who took strong ground against the Writs of Assistance, arguing that they were not only arbitrary and despotic in their operation, but unconstitutional in their imposition on the Colony, since they were irreconcilable with the Colonial charters and a violation of the rights and prerogatives of the people. Rather than uphold them as a Crown officer, Otis resigned his post of Advocate-General, and became a fervent pleader of the popular cause and denouncer of the legal processes by which the Crown sought to impose, with its authority, its obnoxious trammellings and restrictions without the consent of and in defiance of the inalienable rights of the American people. Otis not only resisted the enforcement by the King's officers of the odious warrants and denounced their arbitrary character, but inveighed hotly against English oppression and all attempts of the Crown and its deputy in the province, the Lieutenant-Governor of Massachusetts, to restrict the liberties of the people and impose unconstitutional laws upon the Colony. The Writs of Assistance were, of course, defended by the representatives of the Crown in the Colony, and on the plea that without some such legal process the laws could not be executed, and that similar writs were in existence in England and made use of there on the authority of English statutes. The pleas against them advanced by Otis took cognizance of the fact that the Writs were irreconcilable with the charter of the Massachusetts Colony, that English precedent for their enforcement had no application in America, and that taxation by the Motherland and compulsory acts of the nature of the Writs did open violence to the rights and liberties of the people and were inherently arbitrary and despotic, being imposed without the consent of the Colonies and to their grave hurt and detriment. In pleading the Colonial cause against the Writs, Otis struck a chord in the heart of the people which tingled and vibrated, while stirring up such opposition to them that the authorities were fain to hold their hand and await instructions from the English ministry as to their withdrawal or enforcement. The response of the home government was that they should be enforced, but little advantage was taken of this mandate in the Colonies, since opposition to the Writs had, thanks to the patriot Otis's denunciation of them, became almost universal; while the people had been roused to a sharp sense of their situation, in view of the tyrannous attitude of England towards the Colonies, and the next step taken by the Crown, under Prime Minister Grenville, in threatening them with the no less hated Stamp Tax. This new fiscal infatuation on the part-of the English ministry strained the relations of the Colonies toward the Crown to almost the point of rupture. It was, moreover, an unwise exhibition of English stubbornness and impolicy, since it revealed the mistake which England fell into at the time of considering the Settlements of the New World as Colonial possessions to be held solely for the financial benefit of the mother country, rather than for their own advancement and material well-being. It is true, that the Seven Years' War, which had been waged chiefly for the protection of the American dependencies of the Crown, had left a heavy burden of debt upon England which she naturally looked to the Colonies in some measure to repay. But the Colonies had ready their argument-- they objected to being taxed without their consent, and without representation in the British Parliament, besides being, as they thought, sufficiently oppressed by the burden of customs' duties already imposed upon them. The spirit of resistance therefore grew, and was ere long to take a more determined and, to England, fatal form, for the Stamp Act, though later on repealed, was passed, in spite of the protests of the Colonial Assemblies and the increasing soreness of feeling in America against the mother country.

The like service James Otis did for the community of the New World in opposing the Writs of Assistance he also did in opposing the enforcement of the Stamp Act--remonstrances suggested by the patriot's love of independence, and which, besides numberless letters, speeches and addresses, drew from the pre-Revolutionist's trenchant pen several able pamphlets, one vindicating the action of the Massachusetts House of Representatives, of which Otis was now a member, in protesting against England's intolerance in laying grievous taxation on the Colonies, and the others upholding the rights of the Colonies in resisting the Crown's misgovernment, as well as its purpose to tax the Colonies to defray some of the cost England had incurred in prosecuting the French and Indian war. In these patriotic services and labors, Otis, as a public man, took an active and zealous part, besides conducting a large correspondence as chairman of the House Committee of the Legislature on subjects relating to the weal of the whole country. Nor were his duties confined to these matters alone, for we find him at this period engaged in controversies first with Governor Hutchinson, and then with his successor, Governor Bernard, both of whom deemed Otis an arch-rebel and incendiary--a man not only without the pale of considerate treatment by lawfully constituted authority in the Colonies, but the object of contumely and loathing by the obsequious loyalists of the Motherland and all who desired her continued dominance and supremacy in the country. History has happily long since done justice to James Otis and seen him in a fairer and far more worthy light--the light not only of a patriot lover of liberty, but an ardent and invincible defender of his country against autocratic encroachment, and a fearless asserter of the principles which have become the foundation stone of the American nation. In his masterful way, Otis was at times heedlessly bitter and inveterate in his prejudices against the mother country and the King's officers in the Colony; but we must remember the strength as well as the ardor of his affection for his native land and the righteousness of the cause he lovingly espoused and so nobly advocated. We must remember also the antagonisms he naturally aroused, and the hatreds of which he was the object, on the part of loyal authority in the Colony which feared while it traduced him. This is shown in the mishap that befell him in a British coffeehouse in Boston, where he was roughly assaulted by a man named Robinson, an ally of the revenue officers whom he had denounced in an article in the Boston Gazette, an attack that left its traces in the mental ailment which afterwards distressingly incapacitated him and shortened his bright public career. He nevertheless lived to see the fruition of his hopes, in the throwing off by the Colonies of all allegiance to Britain and take part himself in the battle of Bunker Hill. The harvest reaped by his country from the seeds of liberty he had planted in his day was such as might well cheer him in the period of mental darkness which fell upon him and regretfully clouded his closing years. Nor was he, in his own era, without regard and honor among those who delighted in his splendid patriotism, in the days of his manly strength, mental as well as physical, and who held him in high esteem as a patriot orator and the staunchly loyal tribune of the New World peoples. In these days of flaccid patriotism and moral declension in public life, his example may well stimulate and inspire. In his wholehearted devotion to the hopes as well as to the interests of the Colonies most notable was the polemical fervor with which he espoused their cause and noble the stand he took for liberty and independence.

Like many men who have attained eminence in public life, James Otis was the victim in his day of detraction and envy. A specially malignant slander was current with reference to him and his father at the period of the patriot's resigning his Crown post of Advocate-General. The motive for throwing up his appointment and pleading the people's cause against the Writs of Assistance, it was at the time said, was the disappointment of the Otis family at the Chief-Justiceship, then vacant, going to Governor Hutchinson instead of to Colonel James Otis of Barnstable, father of our hero. This aspersion of the fair name of the Otises as patriots and high-minded gentlemen, and the lying assertion that it was this disappointment that led the Otises, father and son, to abandon the Crown's side for that of the people, was cruelly false, and especially so as Hutchinson, who got the post, repeats the falsehood in his "History of Massachusetts" in explanation of the Otises turning their coats and becoming partisans of the popular cause. Nothing could well be more unjust and untrue, for both men were of far too honorable a character and too ardently patriotic to justify the slander and give even the slightest color to the misrepresentation. Were it necessary more emphatically to characterize the slander as false, one might confidently point to the happy relations of the Otises with the other patriots of the time--to men of the stamp of the two Adams statesmen, to Hancock, Randolph, Warren, and other leaders of the Revolutionary era, as well as to the contemporary repute and influence of both men in the heroic annals of the Colonial period. The times were indeed trying and critical, and at the outset of the movement for independence and relief from the irritating aggressions of the Crown, the attitude, we may be sure, was closely watched and not over truthfully reported, of men of influence who took the patriot side and helped on the great cause which was afterwards to be gloriously and triumphantly crowned.

But we pass on to relate, in a few brief words, what remains yet to be told of James Otis's career, and of the pathetic declining days of the hero and his tragic end. While mind and body were intact and working perfectly in unison, Otis continued to give himself heart and soul to the cause he had so patriotically and zealously espoused. Even when his malady showed itself, there were brief returns of useful activity and old-time mental alertness, only, however, to be followed by sad relapses into the eclipse-period of his powers. At periods of respite from his ailment, Otis took part fitfully in his duties as member of the Massachusetts Legislature, of which body he had been Speaker, and did what he could to further the work of legislation. He also at this time appeared once or twice as an advocate in Court, and also continued his correspondence in Committee of the General Assembly with prominent men in the other Colonies, seeking successfully cooperation with them in the great drama of the time. But for the most part we now find him a considerately cared-for guest of his old-time friend, Colonel Samuel Osgood, at the latter's farmhouse at Andover. Here the distinguished pre-Revolutionist had phenomenal premonitions of the coming manner of his death, related to his sister, Mrs. Warren, to whom the patriot on more than one occasion said, that when God in his Providence should take him hence into the eternal world, he hoped it would be by a stroke of lightning! This tragic fate was ere long to be his, for on the afternoon of May 23rd, 1783, when Otis was standing amid a family group at the door of the Osgood homestead at Andover, a bolt from the blue flashed down from aloft and felled the hero to the ground. Death was instantaneous, and happily it left no mark or contortion on his body, while his features had the repose and placidity of seeming sleep. Thus passed the hero from the scenes of earth, and in a sense fitly, for the period was that which saw the close of the drama of the Revolution he had been instrumental in bringing about, and the departure from the soil of the new-born Republic of the last of the English soldiery.

[3]Historian, Biographer, Essayist, Author of a "Precis of English History," a "Continuation of Grecian History," etc., and for many years Editor of Self-Culture Magazine.--The Publishers.

JAMES OTIS ON THE WRITS OF ASSISTANCE February, 1761.

May it please your Honours: I was desired by one of the court to look into the (law) books, and consider the question now before them concerning Writs of Assistance. I have accordingly considered it, and now appear not only in obedience to your order, but likewise in behalf of the inhabitants of this town, who have presented another petition, and out of regard to the liberties of the subject. And I take this opportunity to declare that whether under a fee or not (for in such a cause as this I despise a fee) I will to my dying day oppose, with all the powers and faculties God has given me, all such instruments of slavery on the one hand and villainly on the other, as this Writ of Assistance is.

It appears to me the worst instrument of arbitrary power, the most destructive of English liberty and the fundamental principles of law that ever was found in an English lawbook. I must therefore beg your Honours' patience and attention to the whole range of an argument that may perhaps appear uncommon in many things, as well as to points of learning that are more remote and unusual, that the whole tendency of my design may the more easily be perceived, the conclusions better descend, and the force of them be better felt. I shall not think much of my pains in this cause, as I engaged in it from principle. I was solicited to argue this case as Advocate-General; and, because I would not, I have been charged with desertion from my office. To this charge I can give a very sufficient answer. I renounced that office and I argue this cause from the same principle; and I argue it with the greatest pleasure, as it is in favour of British liberty, at a time when we hear the greatest monarch upon earth declaring from his throne that he glories in the name of Briton and that the privileges of his people are dearer to him than the most valuable prerogatives of his crown; and as it is in opposition to a kind of power, the exercise of which in former periods of history cost one king of England his head and another his crown, I have taken more pains in this cause than I ever will take again, although my engaging in this and another popular cause has raised much resentment. But I think I can sincerely declare that I cheerfully submit myself to every odious name for conscience' sake; and from my soul I despise all those whose guilt, malice, or folly has made them my foes. Let the consequences be what they will, I am determined to proceed. The only principles of public conduct that are worthy of a gentleman or a man are to sacrifice estate, ease, health, and applause, and even life, to the sacred calls of his country. These manly sentiments, in private life, make good citizens; in public life, the patriot and the hero. I do not say that, when brought to the test, I shall be invincible. I pray God I may never be brought to the melancholy trial; but if ever I should, it will then be known how far I can reduce to practice principles which I know to be founded in truth. In the meantime, I will proceed to the subject of this writ.

In the first place, may it please your honours, I will admit that writs of one kind may be legal; that is, special writs, directed to special officers, and to search certain houses, etc., specially set forth in the writ, may be granted by the Court of Exchequer at home, upon oath made before the Lord Treasurer by the person who asks it, that he suspects such goods to be concealed in those very places he desires to search. The Act of 14 Charles II., which Mr. Gridley[4] mentions, proves this. And in this light the writ appears like a warrant from a Justice of the Peace to search for stolen goods. Your honours will find in the old books concerning the office of a Justice of the Peace, precedents of general warrants to search suspected houses. But in more modern books you will find only special warrants to search such and such houses, specially named, in which the complainant has before sworn that he suspects his goods are concealed; and will find it adjudged that special warrants only are legal. In the same manner I rely on it, that the writ prayed for in this petition is illegal. It is a power that places the liberty of every man in the hands of every petty officer. I say, I admit that special Writs of Assistance, to search special places, may be granted to certain persons on oath; but I deny that the writ now prayed for can be granted, for I beg leave to make some observations on the writ itself, before I proceed to other Acts of Parliament. In the first place, the writ is universal, being directed "to all and singular justices, sheriffs, constables, and all other officers and subjects"; so that, in short, it is directed to every subject in the King's domains. Every one with this writ may be a tyrant; if this commission be legal, a tyrant in a legal manner, also, may control, imprison, or murder any one within the realm. In the next place, it is perpetual; there is no return. A man is accountable to no person for his doings. Every man may reign secure in his petty tyranny, and spread terror and desolation around him [until the trump of the Archangel shall excite different emotions in his soul]. In the third place, a person with this writ, in the daytime, may enter all houses, shops, etc., at will, and command all to assist him. Fourthly, by this writ not only deputies, etc., but even their menial servants, are allowed to lord it over us. [What is this but to have the curse of Canaan with a witness on us: t o be the servants of servants, the most despicable of God's creation?] Now one of the most essential branches of English liberty is the freedom of one's house. A man's house is his castle; and whilst he is quiet, he is as well guarded as a prince in his castle. This writ, if it should be declared legal, would totally annihilate this privilege. Custom-house officers may enter our houses when they please; we are commanded to permit their entry. Their menial servants may enter, may break locks, bars, and everything in their way; and whether they break through malice or revenge, no man, no court can inquire. Bare suspicion without oath is sufficient. This wanton exercise of this power is not a chimerical suggestion of a heated brain. I will mention some facts. Mr. Pew had one of these writs, and when Mr. Ware succeeded him, he endorsed this writ over to Mr. Ware, so that these writs are negotiable from one officer to another; and so your Honours have no opportunity of judging the persons to whom this vast power is delegated. Another instance is this: Mr. Justice Walley had called this same Mr. Ware before him, by a constable, for a breach of the Sabbath-day Acts, or that of profane swearing. As soon as he had finished, Mr. Ware asked him if he had done. He replied, "Yes." "Well, then," said Mr. Ware, "I will show you a little of my power. I command you to permit me to search your house for uncustomed goods," and went on to search the house from garret to cellar; and then served the constable in the same manner! But to show another absurdity in this writ, if it should be established, I insist upon it every person, by the 14 Charles II., has this power as well as the Custom-house officers. The words are, "it shall be lawful for any person or persons authorized, etc." What a scene does this open! Every man prompted by revenge, ill-humor or wantonness to inspect the inside of his neighbour's house, may get a Writ of Assistance. Others will ask it from self defence; one arbitrary exertion will provoke another, until society be involved in tumult and in blood!

Again, these writs are not returned. Writs, in their nature, are temporary things. When the purposes for which they are issued are answered, they exist no more; but these live forever; no one can be called to account. Thus reason and the constitution are both against this writ. Let us see what authority there is for it. Not more than one instance can be found of it in all our law-books; and that was in the zenith of arbitrary power, namely, in the reign of Charles II., when star-chamber powers were pushed to extremity by some ignorant clerk of the exchequer. But had this writ been in any book whatever, it would have been illegal. All precedents are under the control of the principles of law. Lord Talbot (the Earl of Shrewsbury, an English peer of the era of William and Mary) says it is better to observe these than any precedents, though in the House of Lords the last resort of the subject. No Acts of Parliament can establish such a writ; though it should be made in the very words of the petition, it would be void. An act against the constitution is void. But this proves no more than what I before observed, that special writs may be granted on oath and probable suspicion. The act of 7 and 8 William III. that the officers of the plantations shall have the same powers, etc., is confined to this sense; that an officer should show probable ground; should take his oath of it; should do this before a magistrate; and that such magistrate, if he think proper, should issue a special warrant to a constable to search the places. That of 6 Anne can prove no more.

[4] Otis's opponent--his legal preceptor--who argued in favor of the Writs.

JAMES OTIS ON THE STAMP ACT. An Oration Delivered Before the Governor and Council In Boston, December 20, 1765.

It is with great grief that I appear before your Excellency (Governor Hutchinson) and Honours (of the City Council) on this occasion. A wicked and unfeeling minister (Earl Grenville) has caused a people, the most loyal and affectionate that ever king was blest with, to groan under the most insupportable oppression.

But I think, Sir, that he now stands upon the brink of inevitable destruction; and trust that soon, very soon, he will feel the full weight of his injured sovereign's righteous indignation. I have no doubt, Sir, but that the loyal and dutiful representations of nine provinces, the cries and supplications of a distressed people, the united voice of all his Majesty's most loyal and affectionate British-American subjects, will obtain all that ample redress which they have a right to expect; and that erelong they will see their cruel and insidious enemies, both at home and abroad, put to shame and confusion.

My brother Adams has entered so largely into the validity of the act, that I shall not enlarge on that head. Indeed, what has been observed is sufficient to convince the most illiterate savage that the Parliament of England had no regard to the very first principles of their own liberties.

Only the preamble of that oppressive act is enough to rouse the blood of every generous Briton.--"We your Majesty's subjects, the commons of Great Britain, etc., do give and grant"--What? Their own property? No! The treasure, the heart's blood of all your Majesty's dutiful and affectionate British-American subjects.

But the time is far spent. I will not tire your patience. It was once a fundamental maxim that every subject had the same right to his life, liberty, property, and the law that the King had to his crown; and 'tis yet, I venture to say, as much as a crown is worth, to deny the subject his law, which is his birthright. 'Tis a first principle "that Majesty should not only shine in arms, but be armed with the laws." The administration of justice is necessary to the very existence of governments. Nothing can warrant the stopping the course of justice but the impossibility of holding courts, by reason of war, invasion, rebellion, or insurrection. This was law at a time when the whole island of Great Britain was divided into an infinite number of petty baronies and principalities; as Germany is, at this day.

Insurrections then, and even invasions, put the whole nation into such confusion that justice could not have her equal course; especially as the kings in ancient times frequently sat as judges. But war has now become so much of a science, and gives so little disturbance to a nation engaged, that no war, foreign or domestic, is a sufficient reason for shutting up the courts. But if it were, we are not in such a state, but far otherwise, the whole people being willing and demanding the full administration of justice. The shutting up of the courts is an abdication, a total dissolution of government. Whoever takes from the king his executive power, takes from the king his kingship. "The laws which forbid a man to pursue his right one way, ought to be understood with this equitable restriction, that one finds judges to whom he may apply."

I can't but observe that cruel and unheard-of neglect of that enemy to his king and country, the author of this Act, that, when all business, the very life and being of a commercial state, was to be carried on by the use of stamps, that wicked and execrable minister never paid the least regard to the miseries of this extensive continent, but suffered the time for the taking place of the Act to elapse months before a single stamp was received. Though this was a high piece of infidelity to the interest of his royal master, yet it makes it evident that it could never be intended, that if stamps were not to be had, it should put a stop to all justice, which is, ipse facto, a dissolution of society.

It is a strange kind of law which we hear advanced nowadays, that because one unpopular Act can't be carried into execution, that therefore there shall be an end of all law. We are not the first people who have risen to prevent the execution of a law; the very people of England themselves rose in opposition to the famous Jew-bill, and got that immediately repealed. And lawyers know that there are limits, beyond which, if parliaments go, their acts bind not.

The king is always presumed to be present in his courts, holding out the law to his subjects; and when he shuts his courts, he unkings himself in the most essential point. Magna Charter and the other statutes are full, "that they will not defer, delay, nor deny any man justice"; "that it shall not be commanded by the Great Seal, or in any other way, to disturb or delay common right." The judges of England are "not to counsel, or assent to anything which may turn to the damage or disherison of the crown." They are sworn not to deny to any man common right, by the king's letters, nor none other man's, nor for none other cause. Is not the dissolution of society a disherison of the crown? The "justices are commanded that they shall do even law and execution of right to all our subjects, rich and poor, without having regard to any person, without letting to do right for any letters or commandment which may come to them, or by any other cause."

ANECDOTES AND CHARACTERISTICS OF OTIS, ETC. OTIS AND HIS FELLOW PATRIOTS.

Professor Hosmer draws the following pictures of Otis and his contemporaries:

"The splendid Otis, whose leadership was at first unquestioned, was like the huge cannon on the man-of-war, in Victor Hugo's story, that had broken from its moorings in the storm, and become a terror to those whom it formerly defended. He was indeed a great gun, from whom in the time of the Stamp Act had been sent the most powerful bolts against unconstitutional oppression. With lashings parted, however, as the storm grew violent he plunged dangerously from side to side, almost sinking the ship, all the more an object to dread from the calibre that had once made him so serviceable. It was a melancholy sight, and yet a great relief, when his friends saw him at last bound hand and foot, and carried into retirement.

"Bowdoin, also, was not firm in health, and though most active and useful in the Council, had thus far done little elsewhere. Hawley, far in the interior, was often absent from the centre in critical times, and somewhat unreliable through a strange moodiness. Cushing was weak. Hancock was hampered by foibles that some times quite canceled his merits. Quincy was a brilliant youth, and, like a youth, sometimes fickle. We have seen him ready to temporize, when to falter was destruction, as at the time of the casting over of the tea; again in unwise fervor, he would counsel assassination as a proper expedient. Warren, too, could rush into extremes of rashness and ferocity, wishing that he might wade to the knees in blood, and had just reached sober, self-reliant manhood when he was taken off.

"John Adams showed only an intermittent zeal in the public cause until the preliminary work was done, and Benjamin Church, half-hearted and venal, early began the double-dealing which was to bring him to a traitor's end. There was need in this group of a man of sufficient ascendency, thorough intellect and character, to win deference from all--wise enough to see always the supreme end, to know what each instrument was fit for, and to bring all forces to bear in the right way--a man of consummate adroitness, to sail in torpedo-sown waters without exciting an explosion, though conducting wires of local prejudice, class sensitiveness, and personal foible on every hand led straight down to magazines of wrath which might shatter the cause in a moment--a man having resources of his own to such an extent that he could supplement from himself what was wanting in others--always awake, though others might want to sleep, always at work though others might be tired--a man devoted, without thought of personal gain or fame, simply and solely to the public cause. Such a man there was, and his name was Samuel Adams."

OTIS AND ADAMS.

Professor Hosmer thus compares Otis and Adams:

"Otis' power was so magnetic that a Boston town meeting, upon his mere entering, would break out into shouts and clapping, and if he spoke he produced effects which may be compared with the sway exercised by Chatham, whom as an orator he much resembled. Long after disease had made him utterly untrustworthy, his spell remained. He brought the American cause to the brink of ruin, because the people would follow him, though he was shattered.

"Of this gift Samuel Adams possessed little. He was always in speech, straightforward and sensible, and upon occasion could be impressive, but his endowment was not that of the mouth of gold.

"While Otis was fitful, vacillating and morbid, Samuel Adams was persistent, undeviating, and sanity itself. While Samuel Adams never abated by a hair his opposition to the British policy, James Otis, who at the outset had given the watch-word to the patriots, later, after Parliament had passed the Stamp Act, said:

"'It is the duty of all humbly and silently to acquiesce in all the decisions of the supreme legislature. Nine hundred and ninety-nine in a thousand will never entertain the thought but of submission to our sovereign, and to the authority of Parliament in all possible contingencies.'"

OTIS AS AN AUTHOR.

In 1762, a pamphlet appeared, bearing the following title: "A Vindication of the Conduct of the House of Representatives, of the Province of the Massachusetts Bay: more particularly in the last session of the General Assembly. By James Otis, Esq., a Member of said House.

"Let such, such only, tread this sacred floor, Who dare to love their country and be poor. Or good though rich, humane and wise though great, Jove give but these, we've naught to fear from fate.

Boston, printed by Edes and Gill."

Instead of copious quotations from this patriotic work, we present the following judgment upon its merits by one best qualified to estimate its worth. "How many volumes," says John Adams, "are concentrated in this little fugitive pamphlet, the production of a few hurried hours, amidst the continual solicitation of a crowd of clients; for his business at the bar at that time was very extensive, and of the first importance, and amidst the host of politicians, suggesting their plans and schemes!

"Look over the Declarations of Rights and Wrongs issued by Congress in 1774.

"Look into the Declaration of Independence in 1776.

"Look into the writings of Dr. Price and Dr. Priestley.

"Look into all the French constitutions of government; and to cap the climax, look into Mr. Thomas Paine's 'Common Sense, Crisis, and Rights of Man;' what can you find that is not to be found in solid substance in this Vindication of the House of Representatives?"

THE TOWN MEETING.

Another important feature in the unfolding of our free institutions, was the system of town meetings which began to be held as early as 1767.

"The chief arena of James Otis' and Sam Adams' influence," as Governor Hutchinson wrote to Lord Dartmouth, "was the town meeting, that Olympian race-course of the Yankee athlete."

Writing to Samuel Adams in 1790 John Adams, looking back to the effect of these events, says:

"Your Boston town meetings and our Harvard College have set the universe in motion."

One held in October of 1767 was presided over by James Otis, and was called to resist new acts of British aggression on colonial rights. On September 12, 1768, a town meeting was held, which was opened with a prayer by Dr. Cooper. Otis was chosen moderator.

The petition for calling the meeting requested, that inquiry should be made of his Excellency, for "the grounds and reasons of sundry declarations made by him, that three regiments might be daily expected," etc.

A committee was appointed to wait upon the governor, urging him in the present critical state of affairs to issue precepts for a general assembly of the province, to take suitable measures for the preservation of their rights and privileges; and that he should be requested to favor the town with an immediate answer.

In October several ship-loads of troops arrive.

The storm thickens.

Another town meeting is called, and it is voted that the several ministers of the Gospel be requested to appoint the next Tuesday as a day of fasting and prayer.

The day arrives, and the place of meeting is crowded by committees from sixty-two towns.

They petition the governor to call a General Court. Otis appeared in behalf of the people, under circumstances that strongly, attest his heroism.

Cannon were planted at the entrance of the building, and a body of troops were quartered in the representatives' chamber.

After the court was opened, Otis rose, and moved that they should adjourn to Faneuil Hall.

With a significant expression of loathing and scorn, he observed, "that the stench occasioned by the troops in the hall of legislation might prove infectious, and that it was utterly derogatory to the court to administer justice at the points of bayonets and mouths of cannon."

JAMES OTIS AT THE BATTLE OF BUNKER HILL.

In the sketch of the life of James Otis, as presented in Appleton's "Cyclopedia of American Biography," an interesting account is given of the part James Otis played in the noted battle of Bunker Hill, in June, 1775.

The minute men who, hastening to the front, passed by the house of the sister of James Otis, with whom he was living, at Watertown, Mass.

At this time he was harmlessly insane, and did not need special watching.

But, as he saw the patriotic farmers hurrying by and heard of the rumor of the impending conflict, he was suddenly seized with a martial spirit. Without saying a word to a single soul, he slipped away unobserved and hurried on towards Boston. On the roadside he stopped at a farmhouse and borrowed a musket, there being nothing seemingly in his manner to suggest mental derangement. Throwing the musket upon his shoulder he hastened on, and was soon joined by the minute men coming from various directions. "Falling in" with them, he took an active part in that eventful contest until darkness closed in upon the combatants. Then, wearied beyond description, though he was, he set out for home after midnight. He afterwards pursued his sad and aimless life, as though nothing unusual had occurred.

INFLUENCE OF THE BATTLE OF BUNKER HILL

Two days before the battle of Bunker Hill Washington had been appointed by the Continental Congress Commander in Chief.

The news of the battle was brought. Foreseeing the significance of the result he said, "The liberties of the country are safe."

Four days afterward Thomas Jefferson entered Congress and the next day news was brought of the Charlestown conflict. "This put fire into his ideal statesmanship." Patrick Henry hearing of it said, "I am glad of it; a breach of our affections was needed to rouse the country to action."

Franklin wrote to his English friends: "England has lost her colonies forever."

THE ANCESTORS OF JAMES OTIS.

Carlyle says: "I never knew a clever man who came out of entirely stupid people." James Otis's great qualities "were an inheritance, not an accident, and inheritance from the best blood of old England." Many years ago, when George Ticknor of Boston was a guest of Lady Holland, at the famous Holland House, in London, her ladyship remarked to him, in her not very engaging way:

"I understand, Mr. Ticknor, that Massachusetts was settled by convicts."

"Indeed," said Mr. Ticknor, "I thought I was somewhat familiar with the history of my State, but I was not aware that what you say was the case."

"But," he continued, "I do now remember that some of your ladyship's ancestors settled in Boston, for there is a monument to one of them in King's Chapel."

James Otis inherited that sturdy New England pride which puts manhood above dukedoms and coronets.

"A king may make a belted knight, A marquis, duke and a' that, But an honest man's aboon his might."

From a race of the true kings of men he was descended, who conquered out of the jaws of the wilderness the priceless inheritance of American privilege and freedom. And while kings at home were trying to crush out the liberties of their subjects, or were dallying with wantons in the palaces built out of the unrequited toil of the long-suffering and downtrodden people, these men of iron were the pioneers of American civilization, at a time, which Holmes so graphically describes:

"When the crows came cawing through the air To pluck the Pilgrim's corn, And bears came snuffing round the door Wherever a babe was born; And rattlesnakes were bigger round Than the butt of the old ram's horn The deacon blew at meeting time, On every Sabbath morn."

COL. BARRE ON JAMES OTIS.

In the debate on the Boston Port Bill in Parliament, April 15th, 1774, Colonel Barre referred to the ruffianly attack made on Mr. Otis, and his treatment of the injury, in a manner that reflects honor on both of the orators.

"Is this the return you make them?" inquired the British statesman.

"When a commissioner of the customs, aided by a number of ruffians, assaulted the celebrated Mr. Otis, in the midst of the town of Boston, and with the most barbarous violence almost murdered him, did the mob, which is said to rule that town, take vengeance on the perpetrators of this inhuman outrage against a person who is supposed to be their demagogue?

"No, sir, the law tried them, the law gave heavy damages against them, which the irreparably injured Mr. Otis most generously forgave, upon an acknowledgment of the offense.

"Can you expect any more such instances of magnanimity under the principle of the Bill now proposed?"

THE GENEROSITY OF OTIS.

He was distinguished for generosity to both friends and foes. Governor Hutchinson said of him: "that he never knew fairer or more noble conduct in a speaker, than in Otis; that he always disdained to take advantage of any clerical error, or similar inadvertence, but passed over minor points, and defended his causes solely on their broad and substantial foundations."

JOHN ADAMS ON OTIS.

But in that contest over the "Writs of Assistance," there was something nobler exhibited than superiority to mercenary consideration.

"It was," says the Venerable President, John Adams, "a moral spectacle more affecting to me than any I have since seen upon the stage, to observe a pupil treating his master with all the deference, respect, esteem, and affection of a son to a father, and that without the least affectation; while he baffled and confounded all his authorities, confuted all his arguments, and reduced him to silence!

"The crown, by its agents, accumulated construction upon construction, and inference upon inference, as the giants heaped Pelion upon Ossa; but Otis, like Jupiter, dashed this whole building to pieces, and scattered the pulverized atoms to the four winds; and no judge, lawyer, or crown officer dared to say, why do ye so?

"He raised such a storm of indignation, that even Hutchinson, who had been appointed on purpose to sanction this writ, dared not utter a word in its favor, and Mr. Gridley himself seemed to me to exult inwardly at the glory and triumph of his pupil."

OTIS COMPARED WITH RANDOLPH.

"The wit exemplified by Mr. Otis in debate," says Dr. Magoon, "was often keen but never malignant, as in John Randolph. The attacks of the latter were often fierce and virulent, not unfrequently in an inverse proportion to the necessity of the case.

"He would yield himself up to a blind and passionate obstinacy, and lacerate his victims for no apparent reason but the mere pleasure of inflicting pangs.

"In this respect, the orator of Roanoke resembled the Sicilian tyrant whose taste for cruelty led him to seek recreation in putting insects to the torture. If such men cannot strike strong blows, they know how to fight with poisonous weapons; thus by their malignity, rather than by their honorable skill, they can bring the noblest antagonist to the ground.

"But Mr. Otis pursued more dignified game and with a loftier purpose.

"He indeed possessed a Swiftian gift of sarcasm, but, unlike the Dean of St. Patrick's, and the forensic gladiator alluded to above, he never employed it in a spirit of hatred and contempt towards the mass of mankind.

"Such persons should remember the words of Colton, that, 'Strong and sharp as our wit may be, it is not so strong as the memory of fools, nor so keen as their resentment; he that has strength of mind to forgive, is by no means weak enough to forget; and it is much more easy to do a cruel thing than to say a severe one.'"

ORATORICAL POWERS

Many of the most effective orators, of all ages, have not been most successful in long and formal efforts. Nor have they always been close and ready debaters. "Sudden bursts which seemed to be the effect of inspiration--short sentences which came like lightning, dazzling, burning, striking down everything before them--sentences which, spoken at critical moments, decided the fate of great questions--sentences which at once became proverbs --sentences which everybody still knows by heart"--in these chiefly lay the oratorical power of Mirabeau and Chatham, Patrick Henry and James Otis.--E. L. Magoon.

THE ELOQUENCE OF OTIS.

Otis was naturally elevated in thought, and dwelt with greatest delight in the calm contemplation of the lofty principles which should govern political and moral conduct.

And yet he was keenly suspectible to excitement. His intellect explored the wilderness of the universe only to increase the discontent of those noble aspirations of his soul which were never at rest.

In early manhood he was a close student, but as he advanced in age he became more and more absorbed in public action.

As ominous storms threatened the common weal, he found less delight in his library than in the stern strife of the forum.

As he prognosticated the coming tempest and comprehended its fearful issue, he became transformed in aspect like one inspired.

His appearance in public always commanded prompt and profound attention; he both awed and delighted the multitudes whom his bold wisdom so opportunely fortified.

"Old South," the "Old Court House," and the "Cradle of liberty," in Boston, were familiar with his eloquence, that resounded like a cheerful clarion in "days that tried men's souls." It was then that his great heart and fervid intellect wrought with disinterested and noble zeal; his action became vehement, and his eyes flashed with unutterable fire; his voice, distinct, melodious, swelling, and increasing in height and depth with each new and bolder sentiment, filled, as with the palpable presence of a deity, the shaking walls. The listeners became rapt and impassioned like the speaker, till their very breath forsook them.

He poured forth a "flood of argument and passion" which achieved the sublimes" earthly good, and happily exemplified the description which Percival has given of indignant patriotism expressed in eloquence:

"Its words Are few, but deep and solemn, and they break Fresh from the fount of feeling, and are full Of all that passion, which, on Carmel, fired The holy prophet, when his lips were coals, The language winged with terror, as when bolts Leap from the brooding tempest, armed with wrath Commissioned to affright us, and destroy."--E. L. Magoon.

OTIS COMPARED WITH AMERICAN ORATORS.

"His eloquence, like that of his distinguished successors, was marked by a striking individuality.

"It did not partake largely of the placid firmness of Samuel Adams; or of the intense brilliancy and exquisite taste of the younger Quincy; or the subdued and elaborate beauty of Lee; or the philosophical depth of John Adams; or the rugged and overwhelming energy of Patrick Henry; though he, most of all Americans, resembled the latter."--E. L. Magoon.

OTIS COMPARED WITH ENGLISH ORATORS.

"Compared with English orators," Dr. Magoon says, "our great countryman was not unlike Sheridan in natural endowment.

"Like him, he was unequaled in impassioned appeals to the general heart of mankind.

"He swayed all by his electric fire; charmed the timid, and inspired the weak; subdued the haughty, and enthralled the prejudiced.

"He traversed the field of argument and invective as a Scythian warrior scours the plain, shooting most deadly arrows when at the greatest speed.

"He rushed into forensic battle, fearless of all consequences; and as the ancient war-chariot would sometimes set its axle on fire by the rapidity of its own movement, so would the ardent soul of Otis become ignited and fulminate with thought, as he swept irresistibly to the goal.

"When aroused by some great crisis, his eloquent words were like bolts of granite heated in a volcano, and shot forth with unerring aim, crashing where they fell."

PHYSICAL APPEARANCE.

In respect to physical ability, Otis was happily endowed. One who knew him well has recorded, that "he was finely formed, and had an intelligent countenance: his eye, voice, and manner were very impressive.

"The elevation of his mind, and the known integrity of his purposes, enabled him to speak with decision and dignity, and commanded the respect as well as the admiration of his audience.

"His eloquence showed but little imagination, yet it was instinct with the fire of passion."

"It may be not unjustly said of Otis, as of Judge Marshall, that he was one of those rare beings that seem to be sent among men from time to time, to keep alive our faith in humanity.

"He had a wonderful power over the popular feelings, but he employed it only for great public benefits. He seems to have said to himself, in the language of the great master of the maxims of life and conduct:

"This above all,--to thine own self be true, And it must follow, as the night the day, Thou canst not then be false to any man."

PORTRAIT OF OTIS.

The portrait of James Otis, Jr., published as a frontispiece to this sketch, is from the oil-painting loaned to the Bostonian Society, by Harrison Gray Otis, of Winthrop, Massachusetts. The painting from which it is taken, now hanging in the Old State House of Boston, is a reproduction of the original portrait by I. Blackburn, to whom Mr. Otis sat for his portrait in 1755. The original in possession of Mrs. Rogers, a descendant of James Otis, may be seen at her residence, No. 8 Otis Place, Boston. But the original is not so well adapted as is the copy to photographic reproduction. The two portraits are identical in feature and character, but the original having a light background offends the camera.

THE SOURCE AND OCCASION OF THE WAR OF THE REVOLUTION.

"The question is, perhaps more curious than profitable, that relates to the source and occasion of the first of that series of events which produced the war of the Revolution. Men have often asked, what was its original cause, and who struck the first blow? This inquiry was well answered by President Jefferson, in a letter to Dr. Waterhouse of Cambridge, written March 3rd, 1818.

"'I suppose it would be difficult to trace our Revolution to its first embryo. We do not know how long it was hatching in the British cabinet, before they ventured to make the first of the experiments which were to develop it in the end, and to produce complete parliamentary supremacy.

"'Those you mention in Massachusetts as preceding the Stamp Act might be the first visible symptoms of that design. The proposition of that Act, in 1764, was the first here. Your opposition, therefore, preceded ours, as occasion was sooner given there than here, and the truth, I suppose, is, that the opposition, in every colony, began whenever the encroachment was presented to it.

"'This question of priority is as the inquiry would be, who first of the three hundred Spartans offered his name to Leonidas. I shall be happy to see justice done to the merits of all.'"

"In the primitive opposition made by Otis to the arbitrary acts of Trade, aided by the Writs of Assistance, he announced two maxims which lay at the foundation of all the subsequent war; one was, that 'taxation without representation was tyranny,' the other, 'that expenditures of public money without appropriations by the representatives of the people, were arbitrary, and therefore unconstitutional. '"

"This early and acute sagacity of our statesman, led Burke finely to describe the political feeling in America as follows;

"'In other countries, the people, more simple, of a less mercurial cast, judge of an ill principle in government, only by an actual grievance; here they anticipate the evil, and judge of the pressure of the grievance, by the badness of the principle.

"'They augur misgovernment at a distance; and snuff the approach of tyranny in every tainted breeze.'"--E. L. Magoon.

STAMPS AND THE STAMP ACT.

During Robert Walpole's administration [1732], a stamp duty was proposed. He said "I will leave the taxation of America to some of my successors, who have more courage than I have."

Sir William Keith, governor of Pennsylvania, proposed a tax in 1739. Franklin thought it just, when a delegate in the Colonial Congress at Albany, in 1754. But when it was proposed to Pitt in 1759 the great English statesman said: "I will never burn my fingers with the American stamp act."

THE STAMPS.

The stamps were upon blue paper, and were to be attached to every piece of paper or parchment, on which a legal instrument was written. For these stamps the Government charged specific prices, for example, for a common property deed, one shilling and sixpence.

THE MINUTE-MAN OF THE REVOLUTION.

The Minute-man of the Revolution! He was the old, the middle-aged, and the young. He was Capt. Miles, of Concord, who said that he went to battle as he went to church. He was Capt. Davis, of Acton, who reproved his men for jesting on the march. He was Deacon Josiah Haynes, of Sudbury, 80 years old, who marched with his company to the South Bridge at Concord, then joined in the hot pursuit to Lexington, and fell as gloriously as Warren at Bunker Hill. He was James Hayward, of Acton, 22 years old, foremost in that deadly race from Concord to Charlestown, who raised his piece at the same moment with a British soldier, each exclaiming, "You are a dead man!" The Briton dropped, shot through the heart.

James Hayward fell mortally wounded. "Father," he said, "I started with forty balls; I have three left. I never did such a day's work before. Tell mother not to mourn too much, and tell her whom I love more than my mother, that

I am not sorry I turned out."--George W. Curtis.

THE BOSTON COMMON SCHOOLS.

The Boston Common Schools were the pride of the town. They were most jealously guarded, and were opened each day with public prayer.

They were the nurseries of a true democracy. In them the men who played the most important part in the Revolutionary period received their early education.

The Adamses, Chancey, Cooper, Cushing, Hancock, Mayhew, Warren, and the rest breathed their bracing atmosphere.

ENGLAND AND AMERICA.

I have already dwelt on the significance of the way in which the Pilgrim Fathers, driven out of England, begin this compact, with which they begin their life in this new world, with warm professions of allegiance to England's King.

Old England, whose King and bishops drove them out, is proud of them to-day, and counts them as truly her children as Shakespeare and Milton and Vane.

As the American walks the corridors and halls of the Parliament House at Westminster, he pays no great heed to the painted kings upon the painted windows, and cares little for the gilded throne in the gilded House of Lords. The Speaker's chair in the Commons does not stir him most, nor the white form of Hampden that stands silent at the door; but his heart beats fastest where, among great scenes from English triumphs of the days of Puritanism and the revolution, he sees the departure of the Pilgrim Fathers to found New England.

England will not let that scene go as a part of American history only, but claims it now as one of the proudest scenes in her own history, too.

It is a bud of promise, I said, when I first saw it there. Shall not its full unfolding be some great reunion of the English race, a prelude to the federation of the world?

Let that picture there in the Parliament House at Westminster stay always in your mind, to remind you of the England in you. Let the picture of the signing of the compact on the "Mayflower" stay with it, to remind you of progress and greater freedom. That, I take it, is what America--New England, now tempered by New Germany, New Ireland, New France--that, I take it, is what America stands for.--Edwin D. Mead.

THE UNIVERSITIES AND THE MEN OF THE REVOLUTION.

You may perhaps remember how Wendell Phillips, in his great Harvard address on "The Scholar and the Republic" reproached some men of learning for their conservatism and timidity, their backwardness in reform. And it is true that conservatism and timidity are never so hateful and harmful as in the scholar. "Be bold, be bold, and evermore be bold," those words which Emerson liked to quote, are words which should ever ring in the scholar's ear.

But you must remember that Roger Williams and Sir Harry Vane, the very men whom Wendell Phillips named as "two men deepest in thought and bravest in speech of all who spoke English in their day," came, the one from Cambridge, the other from Oxford; and that Sam Adams and Jefferson, the two men whom he named as preeminent, in the early days of the republic, for their trust in the people, were the sons of Harvard and William and Mary. John Adams and John Hancock and James Otis and Joseph Warren, the great Boston leaders in the Revolution, were all Harvard men, like Samuel Adams; and you will remember how many of the great Virginians were, like Jefferson, sons of William and Mary.

And never was a revolution so completely led by scholars as the great Puritan Revolution which planted New England and established the English commonwealth.

No. Scholars have often enough been cowards and trimmers.

But from the days when Moses, learned in all the wisdom of the Egyptians, brought his people up out of bondage, and Paul, who had sat at the feet of

Gamaliel, preached Christ, and Wyclif and Luther preached Reformation, to the time when Eliot and Hampden and Pym and Cromwell and Milton and Vane, all scholars of Oxford and Cambridge, worked for English commonwealth, to the time of Jefferson and Samuel Adams and the time of Emerson and Sumner and Gladstone, scholars have been leaders and heroes too.--Edwin D. Mead.

EARL PERCY AND YANKEE DOODLE.

Earl Percy was the son of the Duke of Northumberland. When he was marching out of Boston, his band struck up the tune of Yankee Doodle, in derision.

He saw a boy in Roxbury making himself very merry as he passed.

Percy inquired why he was so merry.

"To think," said the lad, "how you will dance by and by to Chevy Chase."

Percy was much influenced by presentiments, and the words of the boy made him moody. Percy was a lineal descendant of the Earl Percy who was slain in the battle of Chevy Chase, and he felt all day as if some great calamity might befall him.

STORY OF JAMES OTIS. FOR A SCHOOL OR CLUB PROGRAMME.

Each numbered paragraph is to be given to a pupil or member to read, or to recite in a clear, distinct tone.

If the school or club is small, each person may take three or four paragraphs, but should not be required to recite them in succession.

1. James Otis was born in West Barnstable, near the center of Massachusetts, February 5, 1725. 2. His ancestors were of English descent. The founder of the family in America, John Otis, came from Hingham, in Norfolk, England, and settled in Hingham, Massachusetts, in the year 1635.

3. His grandson, John Otis, was born in 1635. He removed from Hingham to

Barnstable, where he became a prominent man and held several important positions. For eighteen years he was Colonel of Militia, for twenty years Representative, for twenty-one years member of the Council, for thirteen years Chief Justice of common pleas, and Judge of Probate.

4. His two sons, John and James, became distinguished in public life. James, the father of the subject of this sketch, was an eminent lawyer. He, like his father, became Colonel of Militia, Chief Justice of common pleas, and Judge of Probate.

5. James Otis, Jr. thus by inheritance, derived his legal bent and love for political life.

6. His mother's name was Mary Allyne, or Alleyne, of Wethersfield, Conn., daughter of Joseph Allyne, of Plymouth. She was connected with the founders of Plymouth colony, who arrived in the Mayflower in 1620.

7. James was the oldest of thirteen children, several of whom died in infancy. Others lived to attain distinction.

8. He was fitted for College by the Rev. Jonathan Russell of Barnstable, and was so industrious in his studies that he was ready in his fifteenth year to enter as a freshman at Harvard in June, 1739.

9. There is grave reason for believing that his excessive devotion to study at this early period, had much to do with his nervous and excitable condition in succeeding years.

10. "Make haste slowly" is the translation of a Latin motto, which parents and teachers ought to observe in the education of children.

11. Far better is it for the student to take time in making a thorough preparation for the great work of life, than to rush through his preparatory course at the great risk of health and strength. Let him aim ever be to present "a sound mind in a sound body."

12. James Otis was graduated from college in 1743, after completing a four years successful course.

13. After graduation he wisely gave nearly two years to the pursuits of general literature and science before entering upon the law.

14. In this, he set a good example to the young men of the present day, who are so strongly tempted to enter at once upon professional life, without laying a broad and deep foundation for future usefulness.

15. James Otis was very fond of the best poets, and "in the zealous emulation of their beauties," says Dr. Magoon, "he energized his spirit and power of expression.

16. "He did not merely read over the finest passages--he pondered them--he fused them into his own soul, and reproduced their charms with an energy all his own."

17. In 1745 he entered the law office of Jeremiah Gridley, in Boston, who was then one of the most distinguished lawyers in the country.

18. He began the practice of law in Plymouth, in 1748, but soon found that he was "cabined, cribbed and confined" in the opportunity to rise in such a small place.

19. In 1750 he removed to Boston, and there finding full scope for his powers, soon rose to the foremost rank in his profession.

20. He justly won the high place so generally accorded him, by his learning, his integrity, and his marvelous eloquence.

21. In acting successfully as counsel for the three men who were accused of piracy in Halifax, he received a well earned fee, which was the largest that had ever been paid to a Massachusetts lawyer.

22. Like James A. Garfield, he kept up a lively interest in classical studies during his entire professional career.

23. James Otis married Miss Ruth Cunningham, daughter of a Boston merchant, early in 1755.

24. The marriage was not in all respects a happy one, partly on account of political differences. While he became an ardent patriot, she remained a staunch loyalist until her death on Nov. 15, 1789.

25. Another reason for the want of complete domestic felicity was the peculiar character of his genius, which, so often glowing, excitable and irregular, must have frequently demanded a home forbearance almost miraculous.

26. The elder daughter, Elizabeth, married a Captain Brown of the British army, and ended her days in England. 27. The younger daughter, Mary, married Benjamin, the eldest son of the distinguished General Lincoln.

28. In 1761, when he was thirty-six years of age his great political career began, by his determined opposition to the "Writs of Assistance."

29. He said with an eloquence that thrilled every heart, "A man's house is his castle; and while he is quiet, he is as well guarded as a prince in his castle. This Writ, if it should be declared legal, would totally annihilate this privilege."

30. "I am determined to sacrifice estate, ease, health, applause and even life, to the sacred calls of my country in opposition to a kind of power, the exercise of which cost one king his head and another his throne."

31. In 1762 he published a pamphlet entitled, "The Rights of the Colonies Vindicated," which attracted great attention in England for its finished diction and masterly arguments.

32. In this production he firmly took the unassailable position, that in all questions relating to the expenditure of public money, the rights of a Colonial Legislature were as sacred as the rights of the House of Commons.

33. Some of the Parliamentary leaders in England spoke of the work with contempt. Lord Mansfield, the great English legal luminary, who had carefully read it, rebuked them for their attitude towards it.

34. But they rejoined, as quoted by Bancroft, "The man is mad!" "What then?" answered Mansfield. "One mad man often makes many. Massaniello was mad--nobody doubted it--yet for all that he overturned the government of Naples."

35. In June, 1765, Mr. Otis proposed the calling of a congress of delegates from all the colonies to consider the Stamp Act.

36. In that famous Congress which met in October, 1765, in New York, he was one of the delegates, and was appointed on the committee to prepare an address to the Commons of England.

37. In 1767 he was elected Speaker of the Massachusetts Assembly. Governor Bernard took a decidedly negative position against the fiery orator, whom he feared as much as he did the intrepid Sam Adams.

38. But Bernard could not put a padlock upon the lips of Otis. When the king, who was greatly offended at the Circular Letter to the colonies, which requested them to unite in measures for redress demanded of Bernard to dismiss the Assembly unless it should rescind its action, Otis made a flaming speech.

39. His adversaries said, "It was the most violent, abusive and treasonable declaration that perhaps was ever uttered."

40. In the debate which ensued upon this royal order, Otis said: "We are asked to rescind, are we? Let Great Britain rescind her measures, or the colonies are lost to her forever."

41. Otis carried the House triumphantly with him, and it refused to rescind by a vote of ninety-two to seventeen.

42. In the summer of 1769 he attacked some of the revenue officers in an article in "The Boston Gazette." A few evenings afterwards, while sitting in the British coffee-house in Boston, he was savagely assaulted by a man named Robinson, who struck him on the head with a heavy cane or sword.

43. The severe wound which was produced so greatly aggravated the mental

disease which had before been somewhat apparent, that his reason rapidly forsook him.

44. Otis obtained a judgment of L2,000 against Robinson for the attack, but when the penitent officer made a written apology for his irreparable offense, the sufferer refused to take a penny.

45. In 1771 he was elected to the legislature, and sometimes afterward appeared in court and in the town meeting, but found himself unable to take part in public business.

46. In June, 1775, while living in a state of harmless insanity with his sister, Mercy Warren, at Watertown, Mass., he heard, according to Appleton's "Cyclopedia of American Biography," the rumor of battle. On the 17th he slipped away unobserved, "borrowed a musket from some farmhouse by the roadside, and joined the minute men who were marching to the aid of the troops on Bunker Hill."

47. "He took an active part in that battle, and after it was over made his way home again after midnight."

48. The last years of his life were spent at the residence of Mr. Osgood in Andover. For a brief season it seemed as though his reason was restored. He even undertook a case in the Court of Common Pleas in Boston, but found himself unequal to the exertion demanded of him.

49. He had been persuaded to dine with Governor Hancock and some other friends. "But the presence of his former friends and the revived memories of previous events, gave a great shock to his broken mind." He was persuaded to go back at once to the residence of Mr. Osgood.

50. After his mind had become unsettled he said to Mrs. Warren, "My dear sister, I hope, when God Almighty in his righteous providence shall take me out of time into eternity, that it will be by a flash of lightning," and this wish he often repeated.

51. Six weeks exactly after his return, on May 23, 1783, while standing in the side doorway during a thunder-shower, with his cane in his hand, and telling

the assembled family a story, he was struck by lightning and instantly killed. Not one of the seven or eight persons in the room was injured. "No mark of any kind could be found on Otis, nor was there the slightest change or convulsion on his features."

52. His remains were brought to Boston and interred in the Granary Burying Ground with every mark of respect, a great number of the citizens attending his funeral.

53. James Otis sowed the seeds of liberty in this new world without living to see the harvest, and probably without ever dreaming what magnificent crops would be produced.

54. When the usurpations of un-English parliamentarians and their allies at home, became as burdensome, as they were unjust he defended his countrymen, in whose veins flowed the best of English blood, with an eloquence whose ultimate influence transcended his own sublime aspirations.

55. He taught, in the ominous words, which King James's first House of Commons addressed to the House of Lords, immediately after the monarch had been lecturing them on his own prerogative, that "There may be a People without a king;, but there can be no king without a people."

56. "Fortunately for civil liberty in England and America, in all countries and in all times," as Edward Everett Hale says, "none of the Stuarts ever learned in time what this ominous sentence means--ot James I, the most foolish of them, nor Charles I, the most false; nor Charles II, the most worthless; nor James II, the most obstinate."

57. It could be said of Otis as Coleridge said of O'Connell, "See how triumphant in debate and action he is. And why? Because he asserts a broad principle, acts up to it, rests his body upon it, and has faith in it."

PROGRAMME FOR A JAMES OTIS EVENING.

1. Music 2. Vocal Music--"Remember the Maine." 3. Essay-- "The True Relation of England as a Nation to the Colonies." 4. Vocal or Instrumental Music. 5. Essay--"Writs of Assistance, and Otis' Relation to Them." 6. Music. 7.

A Stereopticon Lecture, illustrating the Famous Buildings and noted features of Boston--The Old North Church, The Old South, Copp's Hill, Bunker Hill, North Square, House of Paul Revere, Site of the Old Dragon Inn, The Old State House, Faneuil Hall, etc. 8. Singing-- "America."

QUESTIONS FOR REVIEW.

Where is the Granary Burying Ground? Why so named? What distinguishes it? Can you give the names of some eminent persons buried there? In what tomb was James Otis interred? What interesting particular was noted when his body was disinterred?

What names are given to the pre-revolutionists, the revolutionists, and the post-revolutionists?

Who is assigned the first place among the protagonists of freedom? Who the second? What is the remarkable thing about the lives of many great men? Will you expand the thought?

When and where was James Otis born? What offices did he fill? When was James Otis, Jr. born? What did he inherit from his father and grandfather? What were transmitted to other members of the family? Give the name of one of these members and her peculiar gifts. What was the name of one of the brothers, and what is said of him?

By whom was James Otis prepared for College? When did he enter College? What is the tradition concerning him? What is said of his College course? What of his excitable temperament? What anecdote is recorded of him? When, and under what distinguished lawyer did he begin his legal studies? What is said of his preceptor?

When and where did he begin to practice law? What are some of the incidents of his early legal career? What is said of the defense by Otis of citizens in connection with the anniversary of the Gunpowder Plot? What is the history of the Gunpowder Plot? When was the first period of his Boston practice? What is said of the non-preservation of the legal pleas and addresses of James Otis? What does tradition say of him as an orator?

When and whom did Otis marry? What is said of the Cunnningham family? What is said of Mrs. Otis? Who comprised the family of Mr. and Mrs. Otis? What is said of the marriage of the elder daughter? What of the younger daughter?

When was the second period in James Otis's life? What is said of him as a rising man? What is said of his scholastic and literary pursuits, etc.? What works did he compose? What did James Otis say about the bad literary tastes of the boys of his time?

Of what is every man the joint product? What were the conditions under which the colonial settlements were formed? What were the feelings of the colonists towards England?

What specific conditions in the development of the colonies may be noted? What were the immediate and forceful causes towards revolution? What is said of the Navigation Act? of the Importation Act? What kind of a question was that at issue? Why?

What is said of the seaboard towns? of the traffic with the West Indies? What period did the epoch of evasion cover? What is said of the iron and steel industry? of ship building?

What did Hutchinson say of his own Appointment? What were some of the personal forces at work? What is said of Hutchinson and others? What slander of James Otis was current? In what language was the case regarding the Writs of Assistance made up? What is said of the trial of the case? Who was one of the eminent spectators? What was the relation of Otis to it?

What did Chief Justice Hutchinson advise in the case of the Writs of Assistance? What is the story narrated of Otis regarding his want of self-control?

What is said of the controversy between Hutchinson and Otis? What resolution did Otis offer in 1762? What is said of his pamphlet on "The Vindication of the Conduct of the House of Representatives," etc.? What is said of the Treaty of Paris? What of the feelings of Americans towards the mother country? What of the utterances of Otis?

What did the Americans claim? What was the reply of Parliament? What is said of the Sugar Act? What of Otis' relations to Lieut.-Governor Hutchinson? Of his relations to the Sugar Act and Stamp Act? Of his relation to an Intercolonial conference? What was Franklin's opinion of this conference? What is the substance of Mr. Otis' letter to the provincial agent? Of Lord Mansfield's view of it?

SUBJECTS FOR SPECIAL STUDY. 1. The French and Indian War. 2. James Otis as an Orator. 3. The English Colonies in America. 4. The Influence of College Men in Public Life. 5. How the American Colonies Grew Together. 6. The Commercial Causes of the Revolution. 7. The Political Causes of the Revolution. 8. Otis Compared with Samuel Adams. 9. The Repeal of the Stamp Act.

CHRONOLOGICAL TABLE IN THE LIFE OF JAMES OTIS.

1725 Born in West Barnstable, Massachusetts, Feb. 5. 1739 Entered Harvard College, June. 1743 Was graduated from Harvard. 1745 Begins the study of law. 1748 Begins the practice of law at Plymouth, Massachusetts. 1750 Removes to Boston. 1755 Marries Miss Ruth Cunningham. 1760 Publishes "Rudiments of Latin Prosody." 1761 Opposes the "Writs of Assistance." 1762 Publishes "The Rights of the Colonies Vindicated." 1765 Moves resolution for Congress of Delegates to consider "The Stamp Act," June. Attends the Congress called to consider "The Stamp Act" in New York, and appointed on the committee to prepare address to Parliament, October. 1767 Elected Speaker of the Massachusetts Assembly. 1769 Attacked and severely injured by Robinson. 1771 Elected to the legislature of Massachusetts. 1775 Participates in the Battle of Bunker Hill, June 17. 1778 Pleads case before court in Boston 1783 Killed by stroke of lightning at Andover, Mass., May 23.

Made in the USA
Monee, IL
07 June 2024

59564032R00066